Top Real Estate Strategies for Success

Imaan R. Correa

All rights reserved.

Copyright © 2024 Imaan R. Correa

Top Real Estate Strategies for Success : Unlock the Secret to Thriving in Real Estate Market Today

Funny helpful tips:

Network actively; connections can open doors to opportunities and collaborations.

Maintain a strong online presence; digital visibility is crucial in today's market.

Introduction

Establishing a successful real estate brokerage involves navigating a myriad of decisions and considerations. This comprehensive guide serves as a roadmap for aspiring brokers, starting with the fundamental choice between a franchise and an independent brokerage. It emphasizes the importance of a clear vision and brand development, offering principles such as clarity, uniqueness, and the addition of a tagline.

Selecting the right agents is a pivotal aspect of brokerage success, and the guide provides insights into creating a structured training schedule, suitable office spaces, and effective agent marketing plans. The discussion extends to services that attract both clients and agents, with a focus on essential software tools to streamline operations.

The guide explores the evolving nature of office spaces, considering state requirements, agent training, and cultural factors. It provides valuable tips on selecting the right office space based on considerations such as culture, services, branding, and image. Staffing becomes crucial for success, and the guide offers insights into hiring strategies, including promoting from within when possible.

Efficient brokerage operations are essential, and the guide delves into setting up streamlined processes and attracting agents effectively. It explores various compensation models, providing insights into creating a balanced structure that aligns with the brokerage's goals. Accurate financial planning is indispensable, breaking down estimated costs and ideal revenue percentages for various elements.

The guide concludes by emphasizing the significance of creating a compelling agent attraction story, designing effective recruiting plans, and implementing the best strategies for recruitment. It serves as a comprehensive resource, equipping readers with the knowledge and strategies needed to navigate the complexities of the real estate brokerage landscape.

Contents

FRANCHISE VS INDEPENDENT BROKERAGE 1
CLARIFY THE VISION FOR YOUR 9
    Starbucks 10
    Whole Foods 11
    Keller Williams Realty 11
    Netflix 12
    Uber 12
    The Beliveau Group of EXP Realty 13
    Step 1 13
    Step 2 13
    Step 3 13
CRAFT A WINNING BRAND 21
    1. Make it easily understandable 26
    2. Be unique 26
    3. Don't distract 27
    4. Add a tagline 28
IDENTIFY THE RIGHT AGENTS 33
    1. Structured Training Schedule 36
    2. Office or Meeting Space 36
    3. Agent Marketing Plan 37
SET UP SERVICES TO ATTRACT AND 43
ESSENTIAL SOFTWARE TO OPERATE A 57
ARE OFFICES STILL NEEDED? 80
    1. State Requirements 84

- 2. New Agent Training 84
- 3. Private and Shared Offices 85
- 4. Brokerage Culture 85
- 5. Services 85
- 6. Branding 86
- 7. Image 86

OFFICE SELECTION 101 89
STAFFING UP FOR SUCCESS 102
   Pro tip: Hire from Within When Possible 111
IDENTIFY BROKERAGE OPERATIONS AND 117
SPLITS AND FEES TO ATTRACT THE RIGHT 126
- 1. Copying Your Current Brokerage 136
- 2. Offering a Compensation Model to Please All Agents 136
- 3. Overestimating Agent Production 136

HOW TO ACCURATELY ESTIMATE EXPENSES 140
   Ideal Percentage of Revenue: 20%-30% 142
   Ideal Percentage of Revenue: 3%-5% 143
   Ideal Percentage of Revenue: 3%-6% 144
   Estimated Costs: $4,800/Yr 147
   Ideal Percentage of Revenue: 2%-4% 148
   Estimated Cost: $0-$24,000/Yr 150
   Estimated Cost: $3,000-$22,000/Yr 151
   Ideal Percentage of Revenue: 2%-5% 151

BROKERAGE BUDGET AND MAXIMIZING 156
CREATE AN AGENT ATTRACTION STORY 165
   Baird and Warner's Villain: Homelessness 169
   Redfin's Villain: Salespeople 169

RE/MAX's Villain: Working Alone 169
DESIGN A SUCCESSFUL RECRUITING PLAN 172
THE 10 BEST RECRUITING STRATEGIES 182
    STEP 1 184
    STEP 2 184
    STEP 3 185
    STEP 4 185
    Instead of giving them the solution… give them a reason to meet with you! 188
BONUS SECTION 192
    (The secret of this script is to start with curiosity in yourvoice) 196
    (If they say YES… Shift your voice to excitement!) 196
THE FINAL LESSON 204

FRANCHISE VS INDEPENDENT BROKERAGE

After working 7 years at a local pizza restaurant, I started my real estate career at the age of twenty-one. So, my entire life skills and qualifications are limited to making pizza and selling real estate.

Starting on a successful real estate team I served 72 families my first year, 104 my second, and 144 my third year! By the age of twenty-seven, I had received every award for sales at my brokerage, including the RE/MAX Hall of Fame.

Like many other agents, seven years into my career, I got the itch… no, not to leave my wife, but to hang my own shingle and start a real estate brokerage. Always the optimist, I threw caution to the wind and partnered with another top producing agent to open our first brokerage.

Despite our individual success as top producing agents, after four years, we failed to grow the brokerage beyond just a few agents. We never reached our goal of the brokerage producing enough profit to support itself without us contributing the majority of our own personal commission income.

After a few years, my partner decided to throw in the towel and go back to being an agent and I chose to shift gears into a leadership role as a CEO and recruiter for a local Keller Williams Office.

That's when things started to click. Recruiting for and managing a 200-agent brokerage opened my eyes to the necessary skills and processes needed to recruit agents and to keep agents productive. Hungry for the understanding of what had prevented us from achieving our goals with our prior brokerage, I quickly absorbed the brokerage training.

In my five-plus year career at Keller Williams, I was recognized as a Black Belt Team Leader for recruiting over 115 agents in a year and operating the #1 Commercial Market Center. I also invested in Keller Williams Franchises and helped other Franchisees reposition their office for success.

Please understand that this book is not to promote any brokerage, company, or franchise. Throughout this book, I will make references to different companies. Each reference is based on my research or personal experiences. I am in no way endorsing, promoting, or degrading any company, brokerage, or franchise.

That being said, before you spend your hard-earned money on your new brokerage you must decide if you want to figure it out on your own or invest in a proven franchise business model.

Having tried both, I can shed some light on the questions you may have when deciding between starting an independent brokerage or buying a real estate franchise. In this chapter, I will share the pros and cons of each from my experience and some questions you need to answer for yourself before making a decision.

Do You Have a Clear Vision and Business Plan for Your Brokerage? If you already have a clear Mission, Vision, and Values for your brokerage, opening an independent brokerage may be the right decision. This is because franchisors (the parent franchise company) have already figured out the vision and the business plan for their brokerages, and they are typically inflexible to changes. Imagine a McDonald's franchisee adding tacos to their menu—that would be a McStake!

Therefore, if your own vision drives you, and that vision doesn't align with the franchisor's vision, you're probably not a good candidate for a franchise. On the other hand, if you have the drive to build a brokerage but don't have a vision or a solid plan, then a franchise may be the perfect solution for you.

Before you make your final decision, there are other things you must consider, like how you are going to attract agents and how much it will cost you to get your brokerage up and running.

The Benefits of Purchasing a Franchise

When it comes to hitting the ground running, franchises have many advantages. Franchises typically have brand awareness, processes, procedures, and software, already in place, which will free you up to focus on sales right away. The main selling point of purchasing a franchise is that having a brand, proven model, and software will allow you to grow your brokerage faster and with less risk than you could on your own. Yes, the upfront costs can be steep, but the benefits and reduced risk can be appealing.

But...the Qualifications to Buy One Can Be Strict

Don't get too excited just yet, because many franchises have qualifications and requirements that you must meet before being considered candidates. This can range from your past real estate achievements to your overall net worth.

Franchises Can Be Easier to Sell

One of the commonly overlooked benefits of a franchise is that there are often other in-company agents and franchisees waiting in line to buy a franchise when a territory opens up. That means you may be able to sell your franchise brokerage quicker and for more money than an independent brokerage once you get it up and running well.

There are other considerations you must make before investing in a franchise, though. For example, does your vision align with the franchise's vision, franchise availability, and the upfront costs? We will cover this in more detail later in this book.

The Benefits of Opening an Independent Brokerage

The unique benefits of opening an independent real estate brokerage are irreplaceable. One of these is that you can be as creative as you choose.

One of the main complaints you will hear about owning a franchise is all the rules you must follow. These seemingly arbitrary rules sustain a cohesive brand and prevent internal conflicts between franchise owners. Franchise rules can sometimes seem petty and will limit your business. Some insist on charging all agents the same splits, maintaining a minimum number of agents and employees, or not allowing you to have office space outside your territory.

If you are operating a franchise, these rules make sense, but you wouldn't be subject to rules like these as an independent brokerage. You can charge your agents whatever you negotiate with them, grow your brokerage as fast as you want to, or seize opportunities by opening offices wherever you choose to, or not at all if that is your plan.

With independent brokerages, you can create a unique brand because the franchise's brand and trademark do not restrict you. This can include your messaging, tag lines, colors, and logos—allowing you to differentiate yourself from the competition further. I love differentiation!

So, if you have the desire to get creative with your brand and marketing, and you don't want to be subject to additional rules, then creating and building your own independent brokerage might be the right path for you.

Do You Have the Systems and Plan to Recruit and Retain Agents?

If you want your brokerage to be profitable enough so you won't have to take listings or work with buyers yourself, then you may be shocked to learn just how much of your time will be spent recruiting agents.

In the successful brokerages I ran, "successful" being the key word here, recruiting was a full-time job. If it wasn't my full-time job, as the owner, I had hired and trained someone to recruit agents.

This is because agent attrition in many real estate brokerages can be greater than 20%. This means if your brokerage has 25 agents you will lose 5 agents each year to competitive brokerages, to agents going out on their own, or to agents leaving the business altogether. Therefore, to grow your brokerage by 5 agents you may have to recruit 10 agents.

Your efforts don't stop at just recruiting agents. Once you have recruited them to your brokerage, you need to retain them by meeting their needs for the next six months, the following year, and ideally, their entire career. This includes providing new agent training, marketing assistance, the latest software, and brand awareness while having competitive splits and fees.

Individually, these are all manageable, but it can become a monumental and expensive task for an independent brokerage to provide all of these services over time. Since your real estate sales skills won't help you here, you will need to create systems for recruiting from scratch if you decide to start your own brokerage.

Franchises provide the processes, procedures, and software systems to fulfill most of these requirements. This allows you to focus on recruiting instead of the never-ending development of new offerings to attract agents. Most franchises also create additional training and events to build a company culture.

It may sound great to have these systems and processes provided for you, but first, you need to look at the overall expense of opening a real estate franchise.

How Much Money Do You Have to Invest into Your Real Franchise Brokerage?

One of the most significant differences between starting your own independent brokerage and purchasing a franchise is the upfront cost. If you open your own independent brokerage, you can bootstrap the startup by starting in a smaller office or co-working space and using over-the-counter software.

Purchasing a franchise is buying a proven business model. Franchisors have standards for everything from office space to furniture, equipment, and software. Therefore, you will spend more money, earlier, to bring the office up to standards for the franchise brand. There are lesser-known real estate franchise business models like NextHome with minimal office requirements that can save you money on start-up costs.

Initial Franchise Fee

Franchises have an upfront franchise fee ranging from $10,000 to $50,000. This is in addition to training and the office buildout. For example, the median total cost of opening a RE/MAX or Keller Williams franchise today is just over $140,000, and the full price can be as high as $350,000.

Royalties

In addition to the upfront cost, franchises also have an ongoing "Royalty" (a fee paid monthly to the Franchisor) ranging from 3-6% of the gross commissions and/or a monthly cost of $25-$400 per month per agent. The Royalty fees are typically passed to the agent and not paid by the franchisee directly.

Commitment

Franchise agreements are traditionally for terms of 5-20 years with renewal fees at each interval. The renewal fees are typically 50% of the Initial Franchise Fee. You will need to factor these expenses into your long-term financial plan.

When investigating the franchise route, the final thing you must consider is the availability of franchise opportunities in your area.

Are There Franchise Opportunities Available in Your Area?

A franchise territory is a geographic boundary around a franchise that prevents another franchisee, within the same company, from opening an office nearby. This prevents competition (from recruiting, not sales) from within their own company. Many of the most common national franchise brands have long ago sold off their franchise territories in most major cities. This can make purchasing a franchise tricky in some areas, especially if you want to be in a great location.

Although franchisors like RE/MAX recently stopped the practice of large franchise territories, they still consider the impact a new franchise might have on their existing franchises.

What Do You Do If the Franchise Territories are Sold Out?

Sold-out franchise territories traditionally leave you with one of three options if you truly want to own a franchise.

1. Partner or become an investor in an existing franchise
2. Join a lesser-known franchise brand that has availability in your area
3. Select an up-and-coming area that hasn't been expanded into yet

Since franchises know that many prime territories are sold out, some offer other arrangements for investors. For example, Keller Williams now permits existing franchisees to partner with agents who wish to run their own brokerage within the existing territories. This allows agents that want to have ownership of a franchise but don't have the capital or territory open to do so.

This change creates a new way for agents who desire the opportunity to build a small brokerage without the considerable expense of a new franchise and the risk of building an independent brokerage.

My Take: Franchise vs. Independent Brokerage

Obviously, most of us that choose a career as real estate agents are really entrepreneurs at heart. Who else would take the chance on a career choice that is 100% commission? I too am an entrepreneur and despite the success I had at Keller Williams, I still had a deep desire to build my own real estate brokerage.

So in 2014, I set out on my own once again and started an independent real estate brokerage from scratch. The new, modern boutique-style brokerage in Boulder, Colorado was wildly successful. We quickly became one of the fastest-growing brokerages in Colorado.

Keep in mind, the experiences I learned from Keller Williams gave us an invaluable advantage when it came down to knowing how to hire employees, recruit agents, and build out beautiful office space. Without that experience I know we wouldn't have had the immediate success entering a competitive market like Boulder.

Fortunately for you, I can share with you the lessons I learned from starting my own brokerage from scratch, growing it to multiple offices, and eventually franchising it out. This path was full of success stories and embarrassing failures, but in the end, the knowledge and experience were priceless.

The Bottom Line

There are many things you must consider when deciding to go out on your own. The decisions you make now may forever affect your personal finances. After you read this book entirely, write out a list of pros and cons to opening an independent brokerage versus committing to purchasing a real estate franchise. In the end, the time you spend doing this will save you hundreds of thousands of dollars down the road.

2

CLARIFY THE VISION FOR YOUR BROKERAGE

One of the biggest mistakes I've made or seen others make when starting a brokerage is not being 100% clear about the type of agents you want to serve, how you want customers to perceive your company, and where you want to take the company in the next 5 years. In fact, partners are often at odds about most of these decisions.

What you need is a Mission: something everyone can agree upon, a worthy cause to invest time and money into.

I want to be clear: If you're setting out to start your own real estate brokerage, the first step is to create your Mission, Vision, and Values Statement (MVV). If you already own or operate a brokerage and you don't have a clear MVV Statement, this is your opportunity to create one. If you're part of another company or franchise that already has an MVV, review it and apply the techniques in this chapter to improve your effectiveness.

This may seem like a tedious task and because of this many founders choose to skip it, only to find later that they are attracting the wrong people to their company or the people they attract are not making the good choices when faced with important decisions.

This is because, quite literally, every decision you make going forward will be made from the perspective of your Mission (why you are doing it), Vision (what it looks like when you achieve it), and Values (what ideals, standards, and rules you will follow to achieve it). Furthermore, your MVV will provide direction for your employees and help your customers differentiate you from your competition.

The Mission Statement

Your brokerage's Mission Statement is a statement of the difference you wish to make in your community, demographic, or industry. It is the opposite of what you see that is wrong. It is the main reason you started your team or brokerage. This is important because it gives you and your organization a singular purpose and something to fight for. It can also inspire your customers and create raving fans.

If we were sitting alone and I asked you, "Tell me why you *really* want to start a real estate brokerage." Would you answer, "Because I wish to educate renters to build generational wealth by becoming homeowners"? Or would you say, "So I could keep more money in my pocket"?

Money Alone is Not a Mission

I know what you are thinking... saving money may be your *real* mission; however, you wouldn't share that mission statement with other people. If this is what you're thinking, I have bad news for you. The real reason always finds its way out to the public and the agents you want to recruit. It will come out in the decisions you make and when you are under stress...and starting a brokerage can be highly stressful. Your mission also needs to inspire others. Being able to buy a new BMW or a vacation home two years from now won't inspire anyone but yourself.

Now, if I am a talented employee or agent interviewing your brokerage, what mission would actually inspire me to join your brokerage? *"I am building a brokerage that educates renters to become homeowners"* or *"I'm just in it to make a quick buck?"*

So if you want a chance of attracting and keeping great agents, your Mission Statement needs to have a message that inspires them. Here are a few examples of inspiring mission statements to get your creative juices flowing.

Examples of Inspiring Mission Statements

Starbucks

"To inspire and nurture the human spirit – one person, one cup, and one neighborhood at a time."

Whole Foods
"Our purpose is to nourish people and the planet."

Keller Williams Realty
"To build careers worth having, businesses worth owning, lives worth living, experiences worth giving, and legacies worth leaving."

How to Write an Inspiring Mission Statement for Your Real Estate Brokerage

Step 1
Decide what it is you stand for. This is the solution or the change you would like to see

Step 2
Determine who (demographic, community, or industry) this problem directly impacts

Step 3
What is the result your solution or change will make in your community?

Step 4
Now write out your statement as follows:

"Our Mission is to [Solve the problem or change] so that [demographic, community, or industry] can [result]."

If you are still having trouble uncovering your Mission Statement, I have found with my coaching clients that if they write a short story about why they initially decided to get into real estate, they will find their "why" within the story.

Once my partners and I had clarity about the impact we wished to make in our community and to the agents we served, we then had to agree on what success looked like when we achieved it. Something that excited us to get up yearly every day and work hard for, and a vision that would pull us through when times get tough.

The Vision Statement

The objective of your Vision Statement is to create a mental picture of what the world will look like when your brokerage realizes the goal you set out to achieve with your mission statement. Don't worry too much about being "realistic" here. Your vision can and should be aspirational and audacious. This is something to strive toward, not necessarily something you will, or even can, achieve.

Why an Audacious Vision Statement is Crucial to Your Brokerage's Success

Big goals require a big vision. An audacious vision statement creates excitement, focus, and commitment.

Bill Gates created the vision for Microsoft to *"put a computer on every desk in every home."* If you met Bill Gates when he was starting Microsoft in his garage, would you have told him his vision was too big?

The Vision Statement gives direction for everyone in the company as to what they are starting to achieve. Think of the Mission Statement as the "Why" and Vision Statement as the "What."

The Vision Statement also guides decisions that will affect your employees, agents, customers, and objectives alike. Once you have it nailed down, every critical decision about your brokerage MUST be made with the Vision in mind.

Examples of Powerful Vision Statements

Netflix
"To continue being one of the leading firms of the internet entertainment era."

Uber
"To make transportation as reliable as running water, everywhere, for everyone."

The <u>Beliveau Group</u> of EXP Realty

"To be the real estate team of choice for buyers, sellers, Realtors, and highly talented professionals who value relationships over transactions*, superior work, and community impact."*

How to Create a Powerful Vision Statement for Your Real Estate Brokerage

Your brokerage's Vision Statement only needs to be one to two sentences. You want it to be easy to remember for your employees, agents, and clients.

That means you need to take the time to make your Vision Statement not only represent what you want for yourself and your employees but your client's interests too. You can (and should) use your vision statement in your marketing and branding, so make sure it sounds appealing, polished, and professional.

Step 1
Begin by thinking about your real estate brokerage three to five years in the future, far enough out that you have time to achieve something big, but not so far in the future that you lose interest.

Step 2
Ask yourself: If both you and your agents and employees work as hard as you possibly can, assuming the market plays along, what could you accomplish? Be specific.

Step 3
Write it down... It's that simple!

A clear Mission and Vision alone will not be enough to lead your brokerage. The last piece to the puzzle is to determine the self-imposed rules that you and your team must abide by to achieve the Vision. These are called Core Values.

Your Brokerage's Core Values

Without Core Values, you may find yourself at odds with your partners and your team members. With Core Values, decisions are weighed against the values before they are decided.

If you wish to have agents and employees in alignment, like a school of fish swimming together, your team members must know the rules that you wish to be followed in order to achieve the vision.

These are not simply the laws set out by the local and national governing bodies. Nor are they the ethics guidelines of the National Association of REALTORS. These are self-imposed ideals, rules, and standards that set you apart from your competitors.

How Core Values Direct Employee Decisions

Think about your favorite restaurant: What if they decided to cut corners and bought lower quality produce but still charged you the same price for your birthday dinner with your family? How would you feel about that? You'd be upset, right? You would probably never go back to that restaurant and might even tell your friends to avoid it too.

This is why great restaurants like Morton's have Core Values (*"We will offer only the finest products—anywhere, anytime, at any cost."*) that help them maintain consistent standards for their food. These Core Values direct the employees not to cut corners when it comes to purchasing food. The same principle applies to your brokerage. Without Core Values, your agents, employees, and even yourself, may take shortcuts to achieve your Mission.

Other companies set extremely high standards with their Core Values. The outdoor clothing company Patagonia's Core Values include *"cause no unnecessary harm"* and *"use business to protect nature."* These values guide them to make repairs to their clothing for free and offer free recycling to prevent their clothes from ending up in landfills. This guiding value helps reduce the impact on the environment and increases customer and employee loyalty. Patagonia's employees and customers resonate with their Core Values.

Core Values can also direct team members to remove barriers or rules to change an industry. Uber, for example, knew that for them to achieve their Vision (*"To make transportation as reliable as running water, everywhere, for everyone"*), they would have to challenge the existing laws preventing people from providing taxi services... and they did!

Uber solved this with the Core Value of "Principled Confrontation." This meant that *"sometimes the world and institutions need to change for the future to be ushered in."*

Examples of Core Values for a Real Estate Brokerage

- **Honesty:** We always tell the truth, no matter how difficult.
- **Quality:** We put pride in our work and stand by it.
- **Learning-Based:** We are constantly learning and growing.
- **Professionalism:** We work and present ourselves with respect and dignity.
- **Efficiency:** We seek not to waste time or money.
- **Win-Win:** Win-Win or No Deal
- **Be the Best:** Through education, service, and effort.
- **Communication:** This is the core of our success.
- **Teamwork:** You are an essential member of our team.
- **Trust:** From our honest communication and follow through.

How to Determine Your Core Values for Your Real Estate Brokerage

The Core Values of your brokerage will come directly from you, the founder. This is NOT a group exercise of what your team members all agree on. This is a direct reflection of the ideals, standards, and rules that you apply to yourself. When we involve others in creating the company's Core Values, we end up with wishy-washy core values that don't provide clear direction when we need it most.

The other reason the values must come from you instead of the team is that you may end up with Core Values that you, as the founder, don't agree with or want to abide by. This will lead to hypocrisy, confusion, and conflict within your organization. Having clear values directly from the founder will provide direction for all team members and clarity when making decisions.

Steps to Create Your Core Values

Step 1

Begin by listing a minimum of 10 Core Values that you have personally followed that have led you to your success in real estate. Dig deep for the personal values that have guided you to the success you have achieved thus far.

Think about difficult decisions you have had to make in the past. Maybe they have saved you from making wrong judgments or revelations about the industry or yourself that fueled your success or gotten you over a plateau. What Core Values have guided you to make the right decisions?

Step 2

Write a short description for each Core Value that reflects what it means to you.

Example of Core Value and Description

Core Value	Description
Honesty	No matter how difficult, we always tell the truth.

Step 3

Narrow the list to remove redundant values. Words like Integrity and Honesty are essentially the same. You can't have integrity if you are not honest.

Your list of Core Values can be as few as five or as many as ten. More than ten can be difficult for your team members to remember. Don't go too crazy with this, but taking the time now to distill your Core Values into a concise statement will pay dividends for many years.

How to Effectively Use Your Mission, Vision, and Values to Lead Your Real Estate Brokerage

Before you finish this exercise and close your notebook for it never to be seen again, understand that learning how to use your MVV, which we cover next, will dramatically increase your effectiveness in leading your team and attract the right customers.

The reason why you should put so much time and effort into your Mission, Vision, and Values is that they will be used in all aspects of running your real estate brokerage, from hiring employees and recruiting agents to attracting clients and managing conflict. Your MVV will also be at the very core of your brand. Ideally, it should be in the back of your mind and every brokerage member's mind whenever they make a decision. Think of your MVV as your mantra.

Using Your Mission, Vision, and Values in Hiring and Recruiting

Your Mission, Vision, and Values will determine what employees you will attract to your company. Your goal is to attract employees and agents aligned with your Mission and repel the people who don't share the same Vision and Values.

To do this, you will post your MVV directly in your job postings for both employees and agents, and you will discuss it in your interview process to determine if they genuinely care about your MVV or they are just looking for a job.

This will weed out the non-believers before they ever join your company. This is the beauty of an inspiring MVV. It will help attract the kind of people that will fuel your long-term success and weed out those who won't. In the long run, this will save you time and money not chasing agents to recruit, admins, and clients or having to let go of people that don't believe in your Mission.

Using Your Mission, Vision, and Values to Attract the Right Customers

You will also use your Mission, Vision, and Values in your marketing, advertising, websites, and listing and buyer presentations. Your MVV is even more critical to your brand than your brokerage name and logo. It will attract clients/customers that also share your brokerage's ideals. This also makes you stand out from the competition and is more memorable.

Take a look at Tesla's Mission Statement: *"To accelerate the world's transition to sustainable energy."* Now, if you are a car buyer that profoundly cares about sustainable energy Tesla's Mission Statement would be attractive to you, right? Even if you couldn't afford one of their cars (yet), you would have a more positive outlook on the company.

Most people believe that customers make purchasing decisions based on features and price, but the truth is it comes from a deeper place. Whether it be an emotional connection, a desire to be a part of a movement, or what the product represents, everything we purchase has a deeper meaning behind it.

When you tap into what that meaning is for your customers, they will be attracted to you and your brokerage. Just like environmentally conscious car buyers are to Tesla automobiles.

Using Your Mission, Vision, and Values to Make Better Decisions

Your Mission, Vision, and Values are the "guiding star" for all decisions, both big and small, for your real estate brokerage.

Think about this scenario: You are buying printer paper, and you are trying to decide between the low-cost 20Lb copy paper or the most expensive 35Lb cotton linen paper. If your Values include *"Quality,"* you obviously would choose the more expensive paper.

However, if your MVV includes; "Don't create unnecessary waste." You may decide to skip buying paper altogether and go entirely paperless. Of course, this decision would also need to be shared with your customers because they may expect you to present them with a formal printed presentation. To prevent them from feeling slighted, review your MVV in your virtual presentations. However, if you included "Don't create unnecessary waste" in your MVV, your customer would not only already know this and not expect a printed presentation, they would also likely share that value with you. After all, part of their decision process in choosing you was probably based on those shared values.

Using Your Mission, Vision, and Values to Overcome Conflict

Your Mission, Vision, and Values can solve or even prevent conflict between agents and customers. This is because you have already made it clear to your employees, agents, and customers what ideals, rules, and values will guide every decision you make as a company.

If you call expired listings, you can relate to this. Not so long ago, as a Managing Broker for my own real estate brokerage, I received a call from an upset homeowner. She began to "explain" that she didn't appreciate that an agent in my company had called her after her home had expired from the MLS.

She felt that the agent was aggressive and too pushy. I explained to her that one of our Values is to *"Challenge ourselves to achieve more"* and that the agent in question was just trying to fulfill one of our company's values.

I went on to ask her if she believed that the previous agent she hired was *"Challenging themselves to achieve more"* for her. She said that her home should have sold, and the reason it didn't sell was that the agent didn't do all she could to sell it. I replied that maybe a more aggressive agent is exactly what she needed, and I set an appointment for the agent to meet with her.

In the future, when conflict arises, and believe me, it's not a matter of *if* but *when* you will simply pull out your list of values and find the appropriate value that addresses the situation. Keep track of how each value is applied and share it in your team meeting to teach your team members how to respond to conflict using the MVV.

The Bottom Line

Taking the time to create your Mission, Vision, and Values will help you attract the right people to achieve success with your real estate brokerage. Your clear MVV will also guide your decisions and help you lead your brokerage and manage conflict.

3

CRAFT A WINNING BRAND
INCLUDING NAME, LOGO, AND COLORS

If you are starting a new real estate brokerage, you want a name and logo that not only stands out but is also memorable, right? Of course, you do! But, the task of coming up with a new and unique logo can be harder than you think.

I experienced this myself, just eight years ago, when I started a real estate brokerage from scratch. My partners and I wanted to create a brand that communicated that our brokerage was boutique, current, and fun. To do this we spent thousands of dollars hiring a professional branding team to help us come up with the winning combination of name, logo, and colors for your brokerage.

Fortunately for you, I am a nerd and I took a lot of notes so I can share with you the process that we followed so you can also come up with the right logo of your own.

Build a Customer Avatar

You may think that creating a customer avatar is a waste of time. Honestly, when I did this exercise the first time I felt the same way. However, after completing this exercise, I found that knowing clearly who my real estate brokerage is trying to connect with allowed me to let go of the desire to please everyone.

Have you heard the quote, "If you're trying to please everyone, you will end up pleasing no one"? The same can be true in branding. "If you're trying to attract everyone, you will attract no one." This is why your name, logo, and colors must be designed to appeal to a specific customer.

Begin by thinking about who your brokerage's ideal customer is. Most brokerages' main focus is attracting real estate agents.

Because without agents, you don't have a brokerage. Yet, some brokerages are specifically designed to attract homebuyers or sellers, like Buyer's Slice Realty, which attracts buyers by offering a commission rebate.

Obviously, you don't want to attract agents and repel buyers and sellers, so at some level your brand must appeal to both. Once you have determined who your ideal customer is, next you will ask yourself the following questions about your customer. Your goal is to develop a mental picture of this person.

What location are they in?
What is their education level?
What are their values?
What do they spend their money on?
What are their hobbies?
What are their interests?
What brands do they like?
What famous people do they admire, and why?

Once you have a clear mental picture of your customer you can begin to develop a brand that will attract them by starting with the name.

Choose a Name

Selecting a real estate brokerage name that will stand the test of time isn't easy, but with a little guidance, you are sure to come up with a winner! When we were coming up with our brokerage's name we originally were coming up with the same old rehashed ideas that had already been played out.

You want your brokerage name to be both original and memorable. This helps not only with customer attraction but later if you decide to expand your brand into new areas, when you purchase your domain, and when you are registering your brokerage name and trademark with the state.

Also, keep your real estate brokerage name short, 1-3 words max. If you use a truly unique word or name, include a subtitle to add a clarification. Apple didn't start out as simply "Apple". They started out as "Apple Computers". You can do this too by adding a tagline like "Real Estate Services" or "Realty" to your name.

When we were coming up with our real estate brokerage brand our marketing expert used the following exercise to get us to think outside the box.

1. Using a large whiteboard, begin brainstorming by writing words that your ideal customer would be attracted to. Things like the city, neighborhood, or state you are in. Features that are familiar in the area like bridges, oceans, lakes, and mountains. Don't overlook lifestyle activities that your avatar would enjoy like skiing, surfing, cycling. Don't be shy, anything goes here. Write as many words that you can think of.

    Continue by writing a list of words that are associated with housing and real estate. This can be words like door, cabinet, avenue, and loft. Keep writing until you have the entire whiteboard filled out.

2. Now that you have a large list of words that will interest your customer avatar and a list that they will associate with real estate, you can begin to narrow the list. Do this by crossing off words that are not exciting to you and or that don't align with your values. From the remaining words, circle the top 4 words in each category to come to your favorite 8 words. Write these words on a separate paper.

3. Erase the whiteboard and write the remaining 8 words in two columns with the interest words on the left and the real estate words on the right.

4. Using the words on the board, combine the words on the left with the words on the right. Your goal is to come up with a

unique and catchy name. Rich Barton, the founder of Zillow, wanted the name to be unique yet familiar. The name Zillow is a combination of the letter Z and the word Pillow. Similarly, the real estate brokerage Trelora is a scramble of the word Realtor.

5. The next step is checking to see if the name is already being used. Begin by Googling the word. Add variations like "real estate" and "realty". Is it already being used in your area? Is it being used in another state?

    Trade Names are registered in each state. This is why you can have a "Smith Real Estate" in both New York City and Chicago, but they are entirely different companies. If the name is already being used in another state then you will have a hard time expanding that name in the future.

    Check to see if the domain is being used or if it is for sale. Barton said the best part of the name Zillow is that he bought the domain for twelve dollars. If the domain is already in use or is more than a few hundred dollars, I suggest looking for a new name.

6. 30% of the population speaks another language. Knowing this, it isn't a bad idea to run your new name through Google Translate to see if the work has a different meaning in another language.

After spending six hours toiling over seemingly endless names we came up with the name Steps. We chose Steps because as real estate coaches we could teach agents the "steps" to become successful in real estate and our agents can help buyers and sellers with the "steps" to buying and selling their home. Steps are also a feature in many homes so we felt that the customers can associate the name to housing.

Next, we had to pick out the best font and logo to represent our brand.

Creating a Font and Logo

After coming up with our real estate brokerage's unique and memorable name, the next point of business was deciding if we would use a font or logo to visually represent our brand.

When done correctly fonts and logos allow customers to quickly identify your brand. They also help them to associate your marketing with your business, whether it is open house signs, online advertising, or your website. This allows the customer to build familiarity and trust with your brand.

Selecting a Font

Some companies spend thousands of dollars coming up with a unique logo, but the truth is you may not have to. Many successful brands, like Tiffany & Co, Coca-Cola, and eBay use a font instead of a logo to represent their brand. A unique font can communicate sophistication, simplicity, and timelessness.

Begin by typing your brokerage's name into a font generator website. These websites can show you what your brokerage's name will look like in over 150 different fonts.

Don't stop there. You want your font to be unique and stand out, so once you have selected your favorite font move your work to a Word Doc. In Word, you can select the same font and adjust the height of the letters and the spacing between the letters to give you a new and unique look.

The downside to selecting a standard font to represent your brand is it may not be possible to copyright it since it isn't a completely unique design. Therefore, if you wish to copyright your font you will need to make some changes. For example, Tiffany & Co's font is based on the font Old Baskerville with some minor changes so they could copyright it so it wouldn't be used by another company.

Some companies, like Nike, use a specific font and logo together to create their brand.

Creating a Logo

The ultimate goal of the logo is for it to be instantly associated with your company. However, designing an outstanding logo is far more complicated than selecting a font.

To help you come up with the best logo for your real estate brokerage I wrote out some simple rules about logo design for you to follow.

Rules of Logo Design

1. Make it easily understandable

You want your logo and name to stand alone without explanation. This means if someone sees your logo they can understand what it represents without you having to explain it to them.

Brands like Target, Apple, and Nike do this well. Both Target and Apple's logos represent the name of the company. Target is a simple target logo and apple is a one-dimensional apple with a bite out of it. Nike's logo on the other hand is a "swoop" that clearly communicates motion. No explanations needed!

Your brokerage's logo should tell the consumer something about the company. Things like the values your brokerage stands for, like Tiffany & Co's blue box. A real estate brokerage's logo could communicate the types of properties, the location, or the types of services it provides.

For example, if your brokerage specializes in beachfront properties, a surfboard or sun-shade umbrella in your logo clearly communicates your location and client demographic.

2. Be unique

A quick Google search of real estate logos will show you endless images of brokerage names with an assortment of roofs, buildings, and skylines sitting on top of the name.

While I think it is appropriate for your logo to represent housing, many of these images are overused.

How is a customer to separate you from the competition if the only differentiation with your brokerages brand is the pitch of the roof above your name?

Instead of a roof, try adding features to your logo that represent the type of housing you sell. For example, if you live in Brooklyn NY, you could use the iconic shape of the front door of a Brownstone in your logo. This is different and clearly represents both housing and New York with one simple image.

3. Don't distract

One of the biggest mistakes companies make is designing a logo that makes sense to them but not to the customer. This can create questions and confusion in the customer's mind and prevent them from working with your brokerage.

One logo that comes to mind is a Japanese Restaurant near me. Their logo used to look more like a toilet with the seat up than the traditional Japanese ramen bowl and lid. As you can imagine, the confusion this caused prevented many customers from eating at this restaurant. Fortunately, they recently updated their logo to a more "appetizing" design.

You can avoid distracting logos by sharing your logo with friends, family, and past customers. Ask them the following questions.

1) What does this logo represent to you?
2) What values does this logo portray to you?
3) What product does this logo sell?
4) How does this logo make you feel?

Feedback can be difficult to hear, especially if you took hours coming up with the design. But remember, a little listening and understanding here can save you from having a toilet seat represent your brand!

4. Add a tagline

It is easy to start daydreaming about your logo being immediately associated with real estate, but that's not realistic because **you're not Apple... YET!** In the beginning, the customers won't immediately recognize your logo as a real estate brokerage.

As I said earlier, Apple didn't start out as simply "Apple." They started out as Apple Computers. So don't worry about helping your branding along by adding a tagline like "Real Estate Services". Like Apple, you can drop it later when your brand is better known.

There are many outsourcing websites like Fiverr and 99 Designs that have design professionals who for a very low cost will create a logo for your real estate brokerage. I caution you that many of these designers reuse their designs over and over again. I found this out when a t-shirt logo I had designed showed up on another man's hat!

This can also make it nearly impossible to trademark. If you are planning on growing your brokerage beyond your city or state, then I suggest spending the money to hire a professional graphic designer to help you create a logo that can be legally trademarked.

Since our goal with our real estate brokerage was to grow it throughout our state and eventually into other states we hired a professional graphic designer to help us with the logo design. After several renditions, we came up with our final font, logo, and tagline. We felt the lower case font makes it memorable and friendly and the roofline incorporated into the "e" clearly communicates housing, but just in case we added the tagline "real estate" in a traditional serif font. The next thing we needed to do was come up with the colors to represent our brand.

Pick The Right Colors

Customers associate company brand colors with emotions and values. Unspoken messaging like color can attract your ideal customers. No company knows this better than Tiffany & Co. Tiffany Blue or "Blue 1837", named after the founding of Tiffany, has long been associated with vibrancy and escape, and it was designed to make the customer feel anticipation and delight.

If you don't believe that colors say something about your brand... I ask you if you are willing to wear a gold coat to your next open house? (The older agents will get that joke!)

With your customer avatar in mind, think about what emotions and values you want them to feel when they see your logo. Review the colors below and the associated emotions. Write down the three to four colors that are your favorite choices.

Color wheel diagrams:

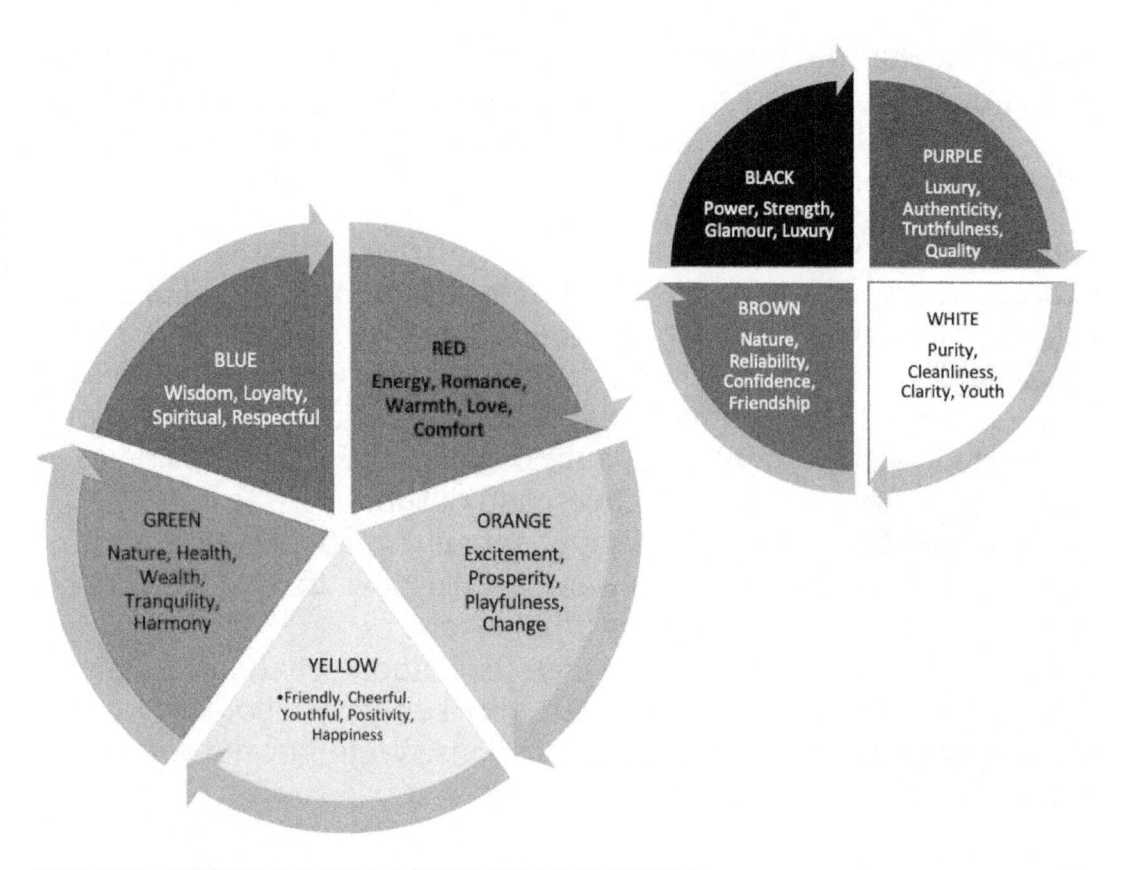

Primary wheel:
- BLUE: Wisdom, Loyalty, Spiritual, Respectful
- RED: Energy, Romance, Warmth, Love, Comfort
- ORANGE: Excitement, Prosperity, Playfulness, Change
- YELLOW: Friendly, Cheerful, Youthful, Positivity, Happiness
- GREEN: Nature, Health, Wealth, Tranquility, Harmony

Secondary wheel:
- BLACK: Power, Strength, Glamour, Luxury
- PURPLE: Luxury, Authenticity, Truthfulness, Quality
- WHITE: Purity, Cleanliness, Clarity, Youth
- BROWN: Nature, Reliability, Confidence, Friendship

COLOR	ASSOCIATED FEELING
BLUE	Wisdom, Loyalty, Spirituality, Respectability, Trust (Dark Blue)
GREEN	Nature, Health, Tranquility, Harmony, Wealth and Money (Dark Green)
YELLOW	Friendly, Cheerful, Youthful, Positivity, Happiness
ORANGE	Excitement, Prosperity, Playfulness, Change
RED	Energy, Warmth, Comfort, Romance, Love
PURPLE	Authenticity, Truth, Luxury, High Quality (Dark Purple)

WHITE	Purity, Youth, Charity, Cleanliness
BROWN	Nature, Reliability, Confidence, Friendship
BLACK	Power, Strength, Glamour, Luxury

Shades and patterns can also change the emotional impact a color can have on a customer. From the three or four colors adjust the shades and narrow them down to two or three colors until you find the ideal color combination that will proudly represent your brokerage.

The focus of our real estate brokerages brand was to be seen as a modern boutique brokerage. We wanted our customers to feel a sense of nature and harmony with the brand. We felt that the colors white, black, and sage green represented the brokerage as a fresh and modern company.

The challenge we found was many sign companies did not have the capability of consistently recreating the correct "sage green" color and at times we had real estate signs that ranged from lime green to an ugly greenish yellow. Yet, I'm sure Tiffany's & Co. has had the same issue.

Favicon

The last part of your logo design is to come up with your Favicon. A Favicon is the small image that shows up in the tab of your browser. The Favicon needs to be 16 pixels high by 16 pixels wide, so your standard logo most likely won't fit.

I have found the best way to do this is to take the most recognizable image from your logo, without the name or tagline and have it sized to fit the browser tab. Google did this by simply using the letter "G" from their logo and adding the rainbow colors. Nike uses a white swoop with a black background. We did the same by taking the "e" from our logo to use as our Favicon.

The Bottom Line

An outstanding brand will not only attract your ideal customers but also the right agents to empower your brokerage to grow beyond your imagination!

Take it from me, there are few things in life more exciting than seeing your real estate brokerage brand showing up throughout your city. Like seeing your child walk for the first time if you find the right brand for your brokerage it too will begin to go off on its own.

4

IDENTIFY THE RIGHT AGENTS

A common mistake that both small and large brokerages make is trying to recruit all types of agents. What I mean by types is new agents, mid-level agents, top producers, and teams. This mistake can end up overwhelming your staff and cost you thousands of dollars to correct.

Unfortunately, I have made this mistake multiple times. Thinking I can build the systems to support the agents once I have recruited them. Let me tell you from experience this ends in disaster.

For example, I once recruited a large team to my brokerage. To do this I offered them a discounted split for the first year, free office space, and additional services from the office staff, that the other agents didn't receive. I justified the deal by telling myself that "We were gaining market share."

Within a few short weeks this sweetheart of a deal got out to the other agents, some who had been with us from the beginning. They felt that it was unfair that the new team was receiving more services and were paying a lower split and fees than they were. "Where's the loyalty?" they asked.

As you can imagine I had to adjust some agreements with existing agents and even offer to provide more services without charging more money, and in the end, the large team left the brokerage at the end of the year when their sweet deal ran out. They left because they said that our brokerage didn't have the systems to support a team of their size. While this was hard to hear, the lesson came through loud and clear. Only recruit the agent types that you are prepared to support.

How do I do this, you ask? Don't worry, I will show you how to focus your recruiting efforts on one specific type of agent that will allow you to scale your business sustainably. Then I'll go over the best compensation plans and services you will need to keep them.

Recruiting Starts With Your "Why"

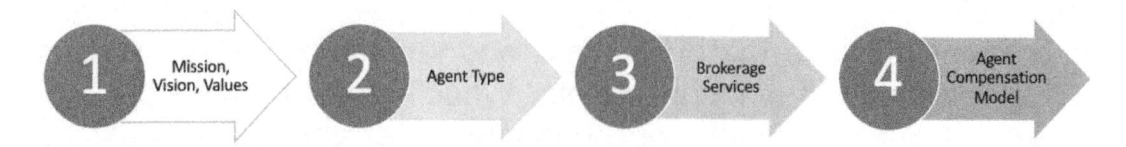

1 Mission, Vision, Values → **2** Agent Type → **3** Brokerage Services → **4** Agent Compensation Model

One of the most common questions I get from new broker-owners is which types of agents they should recruit. I always answer the same way: You're asking the wrong question. Instead, ask yourself what type of agent is my brokerage most likely to attract?"

The first step to uncovering which agents will be attracted to your brokerage is to reflect on "WHY" you decided to build it in the first place. As with any big step you take with your brokerage, the answer lies in your Mission, Vision, and Values. If you haven't worked on your MVV yet, you have no business recruiting anyone.

Your brokerage's Mission, Vision, and Values communicate to your customers, employees, and potential agents why your brokerage exists and how it is different from the competition. This message is specifically designed to attract the agents aligned with your views and repel the agents that aren't. You don't want to waste your time with agents that don't align with your company's vision, do you?

Of course, understanding which types of agents you are likely to attract is only the first step in the process. If you want the agents you recruit to stick with you, you need to clearly understand the services and compensation models they need to thrive.

How To Build a Brokerage with New, Newer, and Low Producing Agents

I know what you are thinking. Who would be crazy enough to build a real estate brokerage with brand new, newer, and low-producing agents? Well, you're listening to him right now. When I opened my real estate brokerage in Boulder, Colorado, I knew it would be challenging for an outsider like me to gain the trust of the producing agents in such a tight-knit community.

I also didn't have a hundred-million-dollar budget to write large checks to attract producing agents as Compass did. What I did have was six years of experience coaching agents as Team Leader and BOLD Coach for Maps Coaching and Keller Williams.

So my solution was to build the brokerage from the bottom up by recruiting and training brand new real estate licensees and newer and low producing agents struggling to get their careers started. The result was outstanding, and I grew the startup brokerage to over 40 agents in the first six months!

Leveling Up With New Agents

After showing the Boulder real estate community that I could guide the most challenging group of agents to be successful quickly in a hyper-competitive market like Boulder, I was able to gain the trust of the established and higher-producing agents. We re-positioned ourselves from attracting newer agents to mid-level agents within a short time, then top producers and teams.

If your brokerage wants to recruit more new or newer agents, you will need to consider what services you will need to provide each and the right compensation plan to appeal to them and support your brokerage.

The 4 Services You Must Provide to Support to New, Newer, and Low-Producing Agents

While new, newer, and low-producing agents are easier to recruit, they are also the most challenging group to get into and keep in production. Many of them lack the knowledge, skills, discipline, and/or mindset to be successful.

Your goal should be to help them achieve a closing with your brokerage within their first 90 days. To do this, you must get them into action quickly. They need to both learn the business and generate leads at the same time. There are four services you must provide if you choose to build a brokerage to support new agents.

1. Structured Training Schedule

If new agents don't have a solid understanding of their job and how their actions are helping customers, they won't have the confidence to talk to people about buying or selling real estate.

To get new, newer, and even low-producing agents producing commission income quickly, you must overcome these two challenges. First, you must quickly grow their real estate transactional knowledge. This includes each task related to working with buyers, sellers and managing a pending transaction to close. The second is the chance to develop skills like showing homes, writing contracts, and giving presentations.

You can provide this by creating a 12-week new agent training schedule that repeats each quarter. The benefit of a repeating schedule is it allows agents to revisit classes as needed, and new agents will feel comfortable knowing that your brokerage is willing to take the time to teach them how to be successful.

2. Office or Meeting Space

More than any other type of agent, new, newer, and low-producers need personal interaction. This is done by having a comfortable place for them to come for the weekly training, monthly team meetings, and when they have a question or are facing a challenge.

I am fully aware that all of this can be online, but if Covid has taught us anything, in-person education is better than virtual. Humans need human interaction, and I believe that newer agents will still prefer a physical office over a virtual office in the post-Covid future.

3. **Agent Marketing Plan**

One of the most significant challenges for all agents is creating and managing an effective agent marketing plan. This is accentuated for agents who don't have experience, listings, or a budget to market themselves to their sphere of influence (SOI).

To solve this common challenge, my brokerage handled their marketing for them. Each month we mailed a postcard to their sphere of influence (SOI). It was a simple postcard marketing one of the brokerage's new listings. This provided more exposure for our listings and presented the new agent as active in real estate to their friends and family.

4. **Leads, Lead Generation Strategies, and Accountability**

Believe it or not, you can run a very profitable brokerage with only newer and low-producing agents. I have a colleague that operates an independent split brokerage model that the brokerage receives up to 70% of the gross commission. In 2019, his independent brokerage profited over a million dollars!

With his unique business model, agents are happy to pay a higher split because, in addition to standard brokerage services and agent training, they provide a steady flow of qualified leads so even a newer agent can produce 1-2 closings a month consistently.

If you are not providing leads, you must provide them with lead generation strategies to generate leads independently. I used the method to teach them about the different real estate lead generation strategies and guide them to pick one based on their Myers-Briggs Type Indicator (MBTI). Using the MBTI, I created different lead generation strategies for each of the personality types. This became the basis for my book 16 Strategies, which is also available on Amazon.

Once they selected their lead generation strategy, I hold them accountable with weekly one-on-one accountability meetings. Even though this was a time-intensive approach, it is the most effective way that I've found to get new agents into production quickly.

Newer Agents Prefer a Low-Risk Compensation Plan

New licensees are worried that the money they saved to start their real estate career will run out before their first commission check comes in. This is because there are many fees they must pay before they can begin their real estate career. In the state of Colorado where I live, the cost just to start your real estate career with real estate education, the association of REALTORS fees, E&O insurance, and MLS can exceed $2,000.

So if you want to have new agents join your brokerage, you must alleviate these fears. One way to do this is to offer to pay for their licensing course. I did this as payback through the first 2-4 closings they had with the brokerage.

Split compensation models also entice most newer and low-producing agents. This is because **split models** are a lower risk for the agent. It allows them to pay fees only when they have commission income from a closing. A benefit of new licensees is that they are less likely to dismiss your new brokerage simply because of a more significant broker split.

Suppose you're building a **transaction fee** brokerage model. In that case, I don't recommend targeting new, newer, or low-producing agents because managing a full training schedule is too time-consuming and expensive to do effectively for a low fee or split. For this model, I would recommend pursuing mid-level and higher agents.

Why You Should Recruit Mid-Level Agents to Your Brokerage

While many recruiters and broker-owners chase top producing agents, the real "bread and butter" of any brokerage are the mid-level agents that produce between 10 and 20 transactions a year. This is because they are more predictable than the other agent types.

Unlike new agents, they require less one-on-one time, and their production is more consistent. They will also stay with your brokerage longer than top producers because they aren't constantly getting poached by other brokerages. Any successful brokerage must have a plan to recruit and support mid-level agents.

The Services That Mid-Level Agents Desire

Mid-level agents that sell between 10-20 transactions a year are doing well for themselves but are usually not producing enough to hire their own assistant to handle their business marketing, listing marketing, and transaction management. Therefore, brokerages that include or provide these services can be very attractive to mid-level agents. Here is a short list of services you can provide to help attract and support mid-level agents.

Brokerage Services to Support Mid-Level Agents

Brokerage Services	Description	Cost
Transaction Coordination	Contract to closing file management	$300-$600/transaction
Showing Service Fee	Fee charged monthly or per listing	$20/month or $75/listing
Signs and Lock Boxes	Sign rental and installation	$75-$150/listing
Open House Signs	Rented and/or installed five	$50-$100/listing
Listing Marketing	Listing marketing packages	$300-$600/listing
Individual Property Website	Individual property website	$50-$100/listing

Listing Presentations	Professional, quality printed listing presentation	$25-$50/listing
Just Listed/Just Sold Cards	100 cards printed and mailed (includes postage)	$100-$200/listing
Listing Photography	Professional listing photography, drone photography	$150-$400/listing

Mid-Level Agents Prefer Predictable Compensation Models

When you create your agent avatar of your ideal mid-level agent, think of a real estate agent in real estate full-time for at least five years. They consistently produce 10-20 transactions each year. They desire to sell more homes but lack the understanding, time, or resources to sell more. They seek brokerages with predictable fees that reward them for their loyalty.

A successful compensation model to attract mid-level agents is the monthly fee model. The **monthly fee** compensation model is more predictable than the split compensation model. You can improve the standard monthly fee model for mid-level agents and show them your appreciation for their loyalty by offering them the option of a longer-term agreement.

Amend your monthly fee agreement to a 3–10-year agreement that guarantees the brokerage fees will not adjust or adjust only moderately (3-5% per year) for the term of the agreement. This will give the mid-level agents the predictability and appreciation they desire, and it provides you the security of a long-term agreement.

Once you have proven your brokerage business model with mid-level agents, it's time to tackle top producers and teams!

When You're Ready to Recruit Top Producers & Teams

Recruiting top producing agents and teams is entirely different from recruiting mid-level or new agents. Unlike the other agent types, most top producer's businesses already rely on their own processes, systems, and employees.

Therefore, it may not matter to them if your brokerage offers a "top of the line" CRM system; because they already have one. Not to mention making a change can be a bigger pain than it is worth for them.

Top Producers Are Less Interested in Services

Top producers and teams are attracted more by opportunity, recognition, and better compensation structures than services.

The fastest way to get the attention of top producers and teams is to offer a fair compensation plan that also allows them to increase their production without increasing expenses or growing their team without taking on undue risk.

Compensation Plans That Entice Top Producers

The brokerage compensation needs of top producers and teams are pretty different from the other agent types. A top producer wants a compensation model that reflects that they are running their own business and making a choice to run *their* business under your umbrella.

Most top producers and team's business plans strive to keep the costs paid to their brokerage to under 10% of their total commission earned. For example, if they made $500,000 in gross commissions, they need to keep their total brokerage costs below $50,000 to afford their marketing, systems, and employees that operate their business.

The simple way to attract top producers and teams is to create a compensation model that allows them to grow their production or team without the brokerage costs rising at a rate more significant than the revenue earned. After all, this is probably one of the reasons they are shopping brokerages in the first place!

This can be achieved by having a compensation model that has a fixed cost component but also doesn't charge a hefty monthly fee for additional team members. This will allow top producers to add new team members and not increase their monthly fixed expenses.

The split with a CAP model is effective for team members because it allows for team growth without the large financial commitment of the monthly fee model. The challenge teams face with all split models is when their team members are successful, the team split can exceed what it would cost them to run their own brokerage… This is also when teams shop around for other brokerages or decide to go out and build a brokerage of their own.

The other compensation model that works for top producers and teams is the transaction fee model with the low monthly fees for team members. This allows the team to use other services provided by the brokerage like marketing, transaction coordination, and software to be used and paid for as needed. This model works because it allows them to keep their costs within their budget and not feel that they are paying for systems and services they are not using, like most other brokerages.

The Bottom Line

Before you make any decisions about your splits and fees, you need to determine the types of services, office space (if any) and the overall budget to operate the brokerage. This is to ensure that you are charging enough to cover the services you are agreeing to provide. Far too many founders offer lower fees hoping to attract agents and then try to add in services they can afford later. Like the tail wagging the dog, this leads to a business model that doesn't have the resources to provide the services, software, and staff to support agents with growing businesses.

5

SET UP SERVICES TO ATTRACT AND SUPPORT AGENTS

Today's sophisticated agents want more from their real estate brokerage than basic file reviews, agent supervision, and commission disbursement. Successful brokerages today are providing more and more services to attract and retain productive agents. So if you don't want your brokerage to get left in the dust, you better step up the services you provide.

Offering high-quality services will not only help you attract more agents but better agents. You can also more easily justify the higher splits and fees you might need to compete in your market.

You may be thinking to yourself how will I ever afford to provide all these services? Well, that is the good news, thanks to technology there are many options from software to outsourcing that make providing brokerage services easier than ever.

In this chapter, I will uncover the complete list of the services that your brokerage may choose to provide, a detailed description of each, and the estimated costs; so you can make the best decision for your brokerage.

Buyer & Seller Leads

Leads are fast becoming one of the most popular offerings of a real estate brokerage today. These are seller and buyer leads generated by the brokerage and referred to the agents for an additional referral fee.

Traditionally agents pay an additional split of up to 30% for these referred clients. If managed correctly, you can make this very profitable for both the agents and your brokerage. Newer agents and agents that close less than 10-transactions are typically attracted to brokerages that refer leads.

Over the last few years, the number of brokerages offering agents buyer and seller leads has exploded. It's easy to see why: Instead of hiring expensive marketers to generate leads, brokers today can just buy leads from Zillow or BoldLeads with one click. The more brokerages offer leads, the more agents expect them.

Some brokerages that have mastered these lead generation systems have added a Lead Manager responsible for generating and managing leads and training and holding the referred agents accountable to follow through to a successful closing.

Why Brokers Are Providing Leads

Your Return on Investment (ROI) providing leads will be directly related to your training and accountability to the agent. Brokerages that do this well can see 3-4 times return on their money. Additionally, there are many talented agents that just need a little momentum in their business, and providing some leads may provide that.

The Costs of Providing Leads

Of course, the cost of providing your agents leads will vary wildly depending on where your brokerage is located. But if you want to provide enough leads to attract and maintain motivated newer agents, then you should expect to spend anywhere from $10,000 to $100,000 per month on leads. Once you throw in a Listing Manager, you can expect to pay another $45,000 per year in salary.

Digital & Print Marketing

One of the most important lessons learned over my 27-year real estate career is that nothing is more important in an agent's business than getting their marketing out consistently. Despite all the available systems and tools, over 80% of agents still fail to follow up with their clients after a sale… Not even a postcard!

These services can include mailing monthly postcards to their SOI and farm area, helping agents with social media content, and creating professional listing and buyer presentations. Your brokerage can provide marketing services through software, outsourcing, or, when you're large enough, hiring a full-time Marketing Manager.

Why Brokers Are Providing Digital & Print Marketing

If you want to add a service that provides value and measurable returns in productivity and profits, then taking over your agent's marketing is the answer. Agent marketing will attract other agents, increase referrals and repeat business from the agents' SOI, and best of all, it helps maintain your brokerage's brand image and standards.

Digital & Print Marketing Benefits vs. Costs Breakdown

Service or Task	Benefit	Cost
Business Cards	Maintain your brand image and standards.	$30 / 500 cards
Social Media Content	Attracts all agents that wish to improve their social media marketing. Maintain your brand image and standards.	$0-$200 month
Agent Video and Video Production	Attracts image-conscious agents that wish to have a professional or polished look. Maintain your brand image and standards.	$100-$500 / video, part-time or full-time Marketing Manager. $20,000-$60,000/Yr
Agent Headshots and Photography	Attracts all agents that wish to have a professional or polished look.	$100-$300 / shoot

	Maintain your brand image and standards.	
Custom Listing and Buyer Presentations	Attracts all agents that wish to have a professional or polished look. Maintain your brand image and standards.	Part-time or full-time Marketing Manager. $20,000-$60,000/Yr
Just Listed and Just Sold Postcards	Attracts busy mid to high-producing listing agents. Maintain your brand image and standards.	$75 / 100 postcards (includes print and mail.) Plus part-time or full-time Marketing Manager. $20,000-$60,000/Yr
Farm Area Mailers	Attracts busy mid to high-producing listing agents. Maintain your brand image and standards.	$375 / 500 postcards (includes print and mail.) Plus part-time or full-time Marketing Manager. $20,000-$60,000/Yr

Listing Preparation and Listing Marketing

If you're trying to recruit listing agents, then offering listing preparation and marketing is a no-brainer. Many high-producing agents are good at lead generation and sales but can fall short when it comes to marketing their listings.

That means you can take a significant burden off their plate by offering to handle all the details of listing preparation like cleaning and staging as well as their listing marketing. This includes photography, video (and video production), sign installation, MLS input, and promotion.

Don't expect your employees to handle all of these details. These services should be outsourced until your real estate brokerage is large enough to support a full-time Listing Manager. Be sure to negotiate volume discounts with your vendors to keep your expenses within budget.

Why Brokers Are Providing Listing Preparation & Marketing

One benefit of providing Listing Preparation and Marketing services is attracting the right agents for your brokerage. Still, there are other benefits you may not be aware of.

Maintain Your Brand Image & Standards

Doing the marketing for your agents ensures that the marketing is done to your real estate brokerage standards and in line with your branding. No more cell phone pics, dark and blurry images, or real estate signs printed with the wrong colors or font. Just this by itself will attract image-conscious home sellers.

Listings Sell Faster and for a Higher Price

When your marketing is done correctly, you will attract more buyers. The more buyers that sell your listings, the greater chance they will sell fast and for top dollar, and this will make your agents look good!

Higher Splits and Fees

Believe it or not, many productive and top-producing agents are happy to pay their broker more to benefit from having all the listing marketing done for them. This gives them the confidence they need to go after luxury listings and gives them back more time to do what they love… make more sales!

Listing Preparation and Marketing Benefit vs. Costs Breakdown

Service or Task	Benefit	Cost
Staging	Attracts busy mid to high-producing listing agents and sells listings faster and for more money. Maintains brand image and standards.	$200-$400 / listing
Virtual Staging	Attracts busy mid to high-producing listing agents and sells listings faster and for more money. Maintains your brand image and standards.	$15-$199 / listing
Deep Cleaning	Attracts busy mid to high-producing listing agents and sells listings faster and for more	$200-$400 / listing

	money. Maintains your brand image and standards.	
Floorplan or Matterport 3D	Attracts busy mid to high-producing listing agents.	$100-$150 / listing
Photography	Attracts busy mid to high-producing listing agents. Maintains your brand image and standards.	$100-$300 / listing
Drone Photography	Attracts busy mid to high-producing listing agents and luxury home sellers.	$100-$300 / listing
Video Production and Editing	Attracts busy mid to high-producing listing agents and luxury home sellers. Maintains your brand image and standards.	$200-$2500 / listing
MLS Input and Management	Attracts busy mid to high-producing listing agents. Maintains your brand image and standards.	$30-$60 / listing or part-time or full-time Listing Manager. $30,000-$45,000/Yr
Listing Promotion: Social Media Channels, Email Blast, Newspaper, TV, and Online.	Attracts all agent types and sells listings faster and for more money. Maintains your brand image and standards.	$0 cost if you are effective at email blasts and social media. $2000-$20,000 / month if you consistently advertise in newspapers, TV, and online.

Transaction Management

If you have a highly accountable group of agents, any task you can take off their plate will increase their productivity. Simply put: If your agents are chasing paperwork, they are not lead generating. Transaction management is an easy and low-cost way to get some of those paperwork chasing tasks off your agents' schedules.

There are two ways you can provide this service to your agents. You can choose to offer this as an a-la-carte service, but I prefer to increase my fees and include it on every file.

Why Brokers Are Providing Transaction Management

Having your brokerage take over the transaction once it has gone under contract will not only free up your agent's time, it will also eliminate the challenge of chasing down paperwork from your agents to complete your required brokerage file.

Since you must have a complete brokerage file on the transaction anyway and pay someone to manage that file, it is easy and inexpensive to add this transaction management to the list of services your brokerage provides.

Transaction Management Benefits vs. Cost Breakdown

Service or Task	Benefit	Cost
Transaction Management	Attracts busy mid to high-producing listing agents. Can be added to the tasks of managing the brokerage file. Agents have more time to lead generate increasing productivity	$200-$400 / file or full-time Transaction Manager. $30,000-$45,000/Yr

Signs and Lock Boxes (Installation, Removal, & Storage)

It may sound simplistic, but providing signs and lock boxes and having them installed, removed, and stored is very enticing to agents. Why? Because what self-respecting agent loves to swing a sledgehammer at a steel sign frame into a frozen lawn? No one, that's who!

Even worse is placing twenty open house signs on busy intersections wearing a black Armani suit in 100-degree weather. Been there… hated it!

Save your agents the pain and embarrassment of having to install listing and open house signs. They will love you for the simple gesture.

To provide this service, you can contract with a local sign company to create, install, remove, and store all your brokerage's signs. The cost is typically $30-$50 for each install or removal.

Why Brokers Are Providing Signs & Lockboxes

Maintain Your Brand Image and Standards

If I had a dollar for every time I saw one of my brokerage signs printed in the wrong color or with the wrong font... I could buy the Miami Dolphins! Most agents are not in tune with the importance of maintaining a brand, and if they can save $10 a sign by having them printed cheaper, they will.

Don't make the mistake I did, and instead include listing and open house signs as part of your services. This will ensure that your brand is always presented with quality.

Promote Your Brand

If your listing and open house signs are branded to your brokerage, you are just paying to promote your brokerage, and the best part is you only pay when your agents take a listing or hold an open house.

Signs and Lockboxes Benefits vs. Cost Breakdown

Service or Task	Benefit	Cost
Sign Installation, Removal & Storage	Attracts busy mid to high-producing listing agents. Maintain your brand image and standards	$60 / listing
Lockbox Installation	Attracts busy mid to high-producing listing agents. Maintain your brand image and standards	$20 / listing
Open House Sign Installation & Removal	Attracts busy mid to high-producing agents. Maintain your brand image and standards	$50-$100 / open house

Meetings and Events

Real estate sales is a social business, and most agents love to socialize. A healthy social schedule will not only increase agent retention but will make recruiting easier. Real estate can also be a lonely business, and many agents are hungry for connection, especially if they are struggling.

Team Meetings

Believe it or not, team meetings are less about education and information and more about building and maintaining relationships and company culture. Coffee and donuts or lunch right after your team meeting can give agents a reason to socialize after the meeting. It also gives them a reason to show up besides listening to you or your Sales Manager talk shop.

Social Happy Hours

A monthly happy hour at a local brewery or trendy bar will make your agents feel like you want to get to know them better and make them feel important. Additionally, these social happy hours are an excellent opportunity to invite agents from other brokerages and an opportunity to check out your company's culture.

Client Events

Client events build your brokerage's brand and provide a reason for your agents to reach out to their SOI and past clients. Many busy agents would love to throw customer appreciation events but lack the time or skills to do them, and some agents with small SOI or past client databases wish to have an event but fear that they won't have enough people show up. Why not give them all a helping hand and coordinate the event for them.

There is no need to do them monthly; quarterly or bi-annually will be enough to keep your agents in front of their SOI.

Meetings and Events Benefits vs. Costs Breakdown

Service or Task	Benefit	Cost
Team Meetings	Improves company culture, education, and agent engagement. Coffee and snacks provided.	Free-$150 / meeting
Happy Hour and Social Events	Improves company culture.	$200 / event
Client Appreciation Events	Attracts busy mid to high-producing listing agents that wish to have more customer engagement.	$1500-$4000 / event

Education and Training

A real estate brokerage that wants to serve agents throughout their career must provide a full suite of agent education and training. If they're not getting it from you, they will get it somewhere else, probably from another brokerage.

Begin by thinking about what phase of agents you want your brokerage to serve. Next, ask yourself: What skills and knowledge do they need to succeed at this phase and push through to the next stage?

If you don't have time for this rhetorical question, I did some of the thinking for you. Below is a shortlist of phases of an agent's career, as well as classes that will support them in that phase.

Review the agent phases below and decide how to provide the proper education and training for your agents.

The Kinds of Education & Training are Brokers Offering

Pre-licensed

People interested in getting into real estate need access to a real estate school. Many successful brokerages either offer an in-house real estate license school or have an affiliation with a real estate license school to refer students to in exchange to promote their brokerage to the school's students. So if your business model includes recruiting brand new agents, then offering pre-license education is a no-brainer.

New and Newer Agents

New and newer agents need a structured training calendar. One that can walk a new licensee through a marketing plan, lead generation strategies, and all the required tasks related to working with buyers and sellers.

Newer agents also need the support of a mentor that they can call to get their urgent questions answered. This ensures that they are doing the right thing and protects your brokerage.

Productive Agents

Busy, productive agents don't want to sit in classes week to week. They only want to attend courses that they can directly apply to their business. Effective agents are attracted to business planning, lead generation classes, and CE credit courses geared towards topics they use.

Top Producers and Teams

Top producers and teams are looking for educational opportunities geared towards the latest systems, tools, and strategies that help them bring their business to the next level.

Try bringing in coaches, trainers, or top producers from other markets to teach your driven agents. Agents outside your market area are more likely to share their secrets without fearing a competitor taking their market share away.

Education and Training Benefits vs. Costs Breakdown

Service or Task	Benefit	Cost
Real Estate License School	Great way to have a consistent source of new agents into your company.	Part-time or full-time Teacher. $10,000-$40,000/Yr
New Agent Training	A must if your brokerage chooses to attract new or newer agents.	Part-time or full-time Trainer/Mentor.

		$10,000-$40,000/Yr
Mentoring	A must if your brokerage chooses to attract new or newer agents.	Part-time or full-time Mentor. $10,000-$40,000/Yr
Prospecting Training	For agents who wish to make more sales and improve their sales skills.	$500-$2000/Training event
Continuing Education and Contract Classes	For agents who wish to be up-to-date with CE credits and contract changes.	$30-$40/Agent
Business Planning	Attracts productive agents who wish to grow and create consistency in their business.	$500-$2000/Training event
Team Building Training	Attracts high-level agents that wish to take their business to the next level.	$500-$2000/Training event

Office Management Services

Let's not forget that there is more to real estate brokerage services than just printing fliers, holding classes, and running team meetings. You still have to fulfill all the state-mandated Managing Broker activities, like agent supervision and file compliance.

Not to mention all the management tasks that come with running a brokerage, such as financial management, reception, and recruiting.

While these services may not be on your company brochure, if you wish to have a successful brokerage, they still need to be managed. So don't overlook the behind-the-scenes real estate brokerage office management services and tasks.

Office Management and Services Benefits vs Costs Breakdown

Services or Task	Benefit	Cost
Reception	Open and close office, answer phones, greet agents and guests	Full-time Receptionist $30,000-$35,000/Yr
Showing Service	Set and coordinate showings and manage feedback	$29/Agent or $20/Listing
Financial Management	Issue commission checks, pay bills, create financial documents	Part-time or full-time Operations Manager $15,000-$42,000/Yr
Broker File Review	Managing Broker reviews each file for legal compliance	Full-time Licensed Managing Broker $40,000/Yr + and/or No Cap and Fees
File Compliance	Brokerage file reviewed for dates, signatures, and disclosure compliance	Part-time or full-time Transaction Manager $15,000-$32,000/Yr
Agent Recruiting	Recruit, interview, and onboard new agents	Part-time or full-time Sales Manager $30,000-$60,00/Yr + bonus

The Bottom Line

At this point, you may be reconsidering your choice to open your own brokerage. If so, you are smart. Opening any business is challenging, and a real estate brokerage is no different. This is exactly why real estate brokerage franchises exist. A good franchise system handles the difficult tasks of running a business and makes it easier for the owner-operator to achieve success faster.

The types of services you choose to offer will ultimately determine the employees you will need to successfully run your real estate brokerage. A common mistake new brokers make is offering too many services when their brokerage is small. This mistake puts too much stress on a young brokerage's limited staff.

To avoid this misstep, you must choose the services that are essential to your business—all while not breaking the bank. One way to do this is to use a combination of software solutions, outsourcing, and hired employees to manage the remaining tasks.

6

ESSENTIAL SOFTWARE TO OPERATE A BROKERAGE

In the past, one benefit of owning a franchise was the ability to have access to top-of-the-line software. These are software solutions that manage agent expenses, commission income, and even lead generation. However, today there are many software solutions that are available to brokerages of any size.

When it comes to real estate broker software, the choices are endless and confusing. This is because many software providers are trying to bridge the gap between one category (like CRMs) to another (brokerage financial management). Even worse, the real estate tech space moves insanely fast these days.

To make your decision-making process easier, I put together this guide to the best real estate brokerage software solutions and categories.

Essential Real Estate Broker Software & Pricing

Digital & Print Marketing Suites

Unless you plan on hiring a Marketing Manager, you will need to provide a way for your agents to create their own professional-looking presentations, postcards, newsletters, flyers, and social media marketing. A robust digital and print marketing suite can do all of this and help maintain your brokerage's brand and quality standards.

Since branding matters more than ever today, software that lets your agents create beautiful, on-brand marketing materials quickly and efficiently is no longer optional.

Digital & Print Marketing Suite Features to Consider

- Branded Custom Templates
    - Fiers
    - Just Sold
    - Just Listed
    - Feature Cards
    - Postcards
    - Printed listing presentations
    - Digital listing presentations
    - Facebook banners
    - Email newsletters
    - Door Hangers
    - Letterhead
    - Thank you cards
    - Open House Materials
    - Social Media Templates

Features to consider:

- Social Media Shareable
- Online Modifiable
- Printable
- Direct Mail
- Direct to Printer

No matter what features you prioritize, a general rule of thumb to follow is that real estate-specific marketing software and apps generally offer a better ROI than general software and apps. Sure, you can make Canva work for your agents, but you're going to have to work at it.

The Best Digital Marketing Suite Options for Brokerages:

Lab Coat Agents Marketing Center
Pricing: Starting at $249 / month for up to 10 users
Ease of use: Easy

EXPLORING THE SCIENCE OF MARKETING

If you want your agents' marketing to succeed on social media *and* print, Lab Coat Agents Marketing Center is a must. It's the first easy-to-use design app created specifically for real estate agents and teams. They offer beautiful real estate-specific templates for social media, open house flyers, open house signs, letters, business cards, and much more. You can even white label the app to include your brokerage's branding.

Breakthrough Broker
Pricing: $13.95 per agent, per month
Ease of use: Easy

Many of you are already familiar with Breakthrough Broker, but you may not know that they offer a Custom Marketing Center for brokerages. Their custom solution allows your brokerage to offer its agents a complete marketing suite that will rival any fortune 500 competitor's for less than the cost of hiring a college graduate.

CORE Listing Machine
Pricing: Contact for pricing

Ease of use: Easy

CORE ListingMachine

CORE Listing Machine (formerly CirclePix) takes the time and hassle out of promoting your listings with a fully automated print and digital marketing suite. Connected CORE Listing Machine pulls details directly from your MLS and creates a complete marketing campaign for each stage of your listing's life cycle, including just listed, open house, price improvement, and just sold.

Financial Management Software

One of the most difficult challenges with running a real estate brokerage is managing the finances. Tracking agent splits, CAPS, and agent billing can quickly become a full-time job. Add in the fact that you may have tens if not hundreds of agents with splits and fees, and without powerful software, this task becomes impossible.

Brokerage financial management software not only tracks agent splits and fees but can also create trending reports, profit and loss statements, and prepare annual 1099 statements. Integration with tax software, credit card servicer, and transaction management software is an absolute must-have feature that will prevent you or your staff from having to waste time doing double entry.

Financial Management Software Features to Consider

- Trust and Escrow Account Management
- Agent Commission Tracking
- Team Commission Tracking
- Agent On and Off-Boarding
- Multi-Office Functionality
- Recurring Billing

- Agent Monthly Fee
- Agent E & O Fee
- Additional Services
- Reports
    - Agent Commissions and Caps
    - P&L
    - Cash Flow
    - Pending Transactions
    - Accounts Receivable
    - Year-Over-Year
    - 1099's and Tax Reports
- Integrations
    - Transaction Management Software
    - CRM
    - Credit Card Provider
    - Quickbooks
    - Email Provider

The Best Financial Management Software Options for Brokerages

Brokermint
Pricing: $59 per month for up to 3 users
Ease of use: Moderate

BROKER MINT

While the basic Brokermint solution may be good enough for a small team or brokerage, you will want to upgrade to the standard ($99/mo) option to have the integration features. Brokermint also offers a white label option, multiple office functionality, and single sign-on with their enterprise package.

Lone Wolf Back Office
Pricing: Contact for brokerage pricing

Ease of use: Moderate

Formerly known as brokerWOLF, Lone Wolf has provided real estate brokerage management software for over 30 years. While Lone Wolf Back Office is a full-featured brokerage management solution, it currently lacks polish when it comes to its useability and is not compatible with Apple.

iBroker
Pricing: $7 per agent
Ease of use: Moderate

iBroker has a clean and straightforward interface for tracking and managing your brokerage's finances. Better yet, their software is optimized for mobile so that your team-style can manage your financials from a phone or tablet. iBroker also integrates with iFranchise software (same company) if you decide to franchise your brokerage in the future.

Real Estate Showing Software

One leading service a real estate brokerage provides is managing showings and feedback on the agent's listings. Sure, you can do this manually, but managing showings after hours and on weekends is not worth the effort.

Therefore, real estate showing software is a must for any brokerage. These solutions allow agents to schedule and provide feedback 24-7 and sellers to accept showings and view feedback instantly.

Real Estate Showing Software Features to Consider

- Mobile Friendly
- Agent App
- Online Scheduler
- Calendar
- Mac and PC Compatible
- In-App Messaging
- Manage Feedback
- Seller Login
- Text (SMS) Notifications
- Integrations
    - MLS
    - Calendar
    - Email

Best Real Estate Showing Software Options for Brokerages 2021

ShowingTime
Pricing: Starting at $45 per agent
Ease of use: Easy

If you have used ShowingTime's App, you already know it is simple to use, and it will save your brokerage the trouble of managing all the showing details. But, with the recent announcement that Zillow has purchased ShowingTime, this may not be your first choice.

Schedulock

Pricing: Starting at $30 per agent
Ease of use: Easy

Schedulock

Schedulock offers email and text notifications along with a mobile-friendly App. Keep your agents informed with in-App agent paging to your entire brokerage.

All-In-One Website/CRM Real Estate Broker Software

Today, nearly every national real estate brokerage offers some type of all-in-one website/CRM. Whether it is kvCORE (EXP), Command (Keller Williams), or booj (RE/MAX), these systems all have one thing in common: they combine IDX capable agent websites, CRM, lead management, and online lead generation systems into one solution.

All-in-one website/CRM solutions were initially designed to support top producing agents and teams specializing in online lead generation. These systems have the unique capability to place ads on Facebook and Google, capture leads through landing pages, and nurture leads with an integrated CRM.

So, if you are planning for your brokerage to go head-to-head with the national real estate brokerages in your area, then you may need to consider one of these top-of-the-line systems.

Real Estate Brokerage All-in-One Website/CRM Features

- SEO Optimized
- Optimized for Mobile
- MLS Home Search (IDX Integration)
- Agent Search
- Map Home Search
- Property Valuation Tool

- Neighborhood and School Data
- Mortgage Calculator
- Lead Capture Capabilities
- CRM Integration
- Featured Listings
- Individual Agent Sites with IDX
- Blog or Vlog
- RSS Fees
- Social Media Links
- Agent Recruiting Page
- Chat Feature
- Artificial Intelligence Autoresponder
- Agent Performance and Conversion Tracking

Real Estate Brokerage All-in-One Website/CRM Challenges

The biggest challenge with these solutions is keeping costs within your budget. The prices of these all-in-one solutions start at a few hundred dollars a month and can quickly grow to thousands a month before spending any money on paid advertising.

Another point is that most of these solutions were built for teams and not for brokerages; they don't allow agents to have stand-alone webpages with their own IDX.

Best All-in-One Website/CRM Options for Brokerages

Real Geeks

Pricing: Contact for brokerage pricing
Ease of use: Moderate

Real Geeks offers an all-in-one solution for agents, teams, and brokerages alike. What I like about Real Geeks is their willingness to customize your brokerage website to your specifications, including standalone agent websites. The tradeoff is that the customized version can become expensive compared to other solutions.

kvCORE

Pricing: Contact for brokerage pricing
Ease of use: Moderate

kvCORE is another early mover in all-in-one website/CRM solutions for brokerages. kvCORE has the distinct advantage of already being used by large franchises. It's a solid system but might not work for every budget. You can learn more in my dedicated kvCORE review on TheClose.com.

Propertybase GO

Pricing: Contact for brokerage pricing
Ease of use: Moderate

Propertybase is a complete all-in-one CRM and marketing solution. What separates them from some of their competitors is the ability for your ad campaigns to be managed by their professional marketing team, removing the learning curve of Facebook and Google ad management.

Chime

CHIME

Pricing: $499 per month
Ease of use: Moderate

Chime combines ease of use with AI technology. They use proprietary AI to help users create an effective marketing campaign and respond to potential customers 24/7. One negative I found with Chime is that it is geared more for team-style brokerages than for brokerages with independent agents. This is because their brokerage site doesn't include individual agent websites with IDX.

Market Leader

market leader.

Pricing: Contact for brokerage pricing
Ease of use: Moderate

Market Leader was once the leader in all-in-one solutions, with many of the top producing agents throughout the country using it to generate and manage real estate leads. Today with many competitors like kvCORE and Boomtown, Market Leader stands out because it provides similar features for about half the price. Like Chime, Market Leader doesn't offer separate agent websites.

Stand-Alone Real Estate Brokerage Websites

The main benefit of having a standalone website is the low cost of getting it up and running. The main features you want to consider are the ability for your website to support IDX Integration, SEO optimization, and that it is optimized for mobile. You can add other features as you grow your brokerage.

Standalone Real Estate Brokerage Website Features to Consider

Must-Have Brokerage Website Features

- SEO Optimized
- Optimized for Mobile
- MLS Home Search (IDX Integration)
- Agent Search

Optional Broker Website Features

- Map Home Search with
- Neighborhood and School Data
- Mortgage Calculator
- Featured Listings
- Blog or Vlog
- RSS Fees
- Social Media Links
- Agent Recruiting Page
- Chat Feature
- Artificial Intelligence Autoresponder

Is a Standalone Website Right for Your Brokerage?

A standalone website may be the right fit for your brokerage if you're not planning on providing and managing leads or if your brokerage focuses on attracting seasoned agents and teams that prefer to have their own website and CRM.

If I was to start a boutique real estate brokerage today and not planning on growing past one location or to compete directly with the national real estate brokerages, this is the way I would go.

Best Standalone Real Estate Website Options for Brokerages:

Custom WordPress Site

WordPress

Pricing: $50 - $5000
Ease of use: Moderate-Difficult

WordPress has come a long way over the years and now powers many real estate websites. IDX integration is easier than ever, and there are a ton of excellent themes that offer agent pages, listings pages, and pretty much anything else you'd need for running a brokerage.

You can try your hand at building your own WordPress site or hire a professional to get you up and running.

Placester

Pricing: $200+ per month
Ease of use: Easy

Great for smaller brokerages, Placester is one of the only affordable brokerage website providers that offer broker and individual agent websites with individual agent IDX integration. This is important if your agents wish to have their own website as a lead capture tool.

Placester is simple enough to use that an agent with average technical skills can build a nice website that integrates with most CRMs, in just a few minutes. The main complaint I have heard from agents is that the Placester website templates are limited and don't allow much customization.

Squarespace

SQUARESPACE

Pricing: $12 per month
Ease of use: Very easy

If you are looking to get your brokerage site up quickly and don't need all the features of a real estate-specific website, then Squarespace may be the right solution. It also supports IDX integration through IDX providers such as Ultimate IDX.

Squarespace is a do-it-yourself solution where you can create and edit your website yourself, or if you are not tech-savvy, you can find several Squarespace developers on freelance websites like Upwork. The overall benefit is you can have your website up quickly for just a few hundred dollars.

Standalone CRM Solutions

CRMs are no longer a nice perk to offer agents. They are now essential. If you don't provide a CRM solution to your agents, you're going to have a tough time recruiting.

The problem, of course, is that there are dozens of CRMs on the market these days, and most have almost identical features for agents.

Yet, your real estate brokerage may have different needs when it comes to a CRM than a real estate agent. So, take some time here to prioritize which features are a must for your real estate brokerage and which are nice to have to make an informed decision.

Real Estate Brokerage CRM Features and Description

Feature	Description
Lead Capture	Capture seller and buyer leads
Lead Automation	Create automated responses to lead inquiries
Lead Routing	Direct your leads to the right agents at the right time
Email Campaign Builder	Create email campaigns within the system

Email Blast	Send a mass email to a large number of contacts
SMS Capabilities	Send and track SMS texts through the system
Auto Dialer	Make and track calls through the system
Voicemail Drop	Send and track a voicemail drop to multiple contacts
Print Mail Capabilities	Send postcards and mailers through the system
Facebook and Google Ad	Place Facebook and Google Ads placed within the system
Video Email	Send video within an email
Agent App	Agent facing app to access CRM and features
Agent Training	Training provided directly to agents
Live Support	Live support for agent questions and problem-solving
Analytics	Tracking agent and brokerage performance

Standalone CRMs Can Keep Your Start-Up Costs Low

You may not want to offer a CRM in the hopes of saving costs. The challenge with letting agents select the CRM of their choice is providing training support and tracking agent productivity if all your agents use different CRMs.

When starting a real estate brokerage, the challenge that I've found is keeping the monthly costs of premium CRMs within the operational budget. A standalone CRM may not have as many features, but it may fit within a smaller budget.

Only Pay for What Your Agents Use

Try starting your real estate brokerage with a CRM provider that offers a per-user fee plan. This is because only about 25% of your agents will actually use the CRM you provide. Many seasoned agents may have their own CRM or one that they prefer more than the one you provide with your brokerage.

A per-user plan will allow you to keep your CRM costs low when your brokerage is small and you need the savings the most.

Best Standalone CRM Options for Brokerages:

LionDesk

LionDesk

Pricing: $25 per month
Ease of use: Easy

(Best Overall) LionDesk is my favorite not only because of the low monthly fee but because it offers many of the same features as CRMs that cost hundreds of dollars a month. Your agents will be able to coordinate email campaigns, send SMS texting, and follow up with leads using the AI-driven text responder, known as Gabby.

Realty Juggler

RealtyJuggler

Pricing: $15 per agent per month
Ease of use: Easy

If you are looking for a great "no-frills," entry-level CRM, RealtyJuggler may be the right option. While it doesn't offer the visual user experience of some of the other more expensive options, it does check nearly every box of the features listed above. RealtyJuggler offers a 90-day free trial and a prorated refund guarantee.

Contactually

Contactually
BY COMPASS

Pricing: $69 per agent per month
Ease of use: Easy

If higher costs aren't a concern for your brokerage start-up, and you are looking for a standalone CRM that actually produces measurable results then Contactually may be a match. Contactually's interface is easy to use, and the automation and workflows are outstanding. These features allow for a higher agent adoption rate than its competitors.

Contactually has multiple payment plans from individual agents to large brokerages, so you may need to contact them about pricing for your specific situation.

Transaction Management Software

Transaction management software will keep your agents organized and your office compliant from a regulatory perspective by collecting and categorizing all the required disclosures, contracts, and managing deadlines.

Transaction management software can also notify the agent, lender, TC, and Broker if items are missing or deadlines are approaching. Best of all, it will ensure that the files are complete so the agents can be paid quicker or even at closing!

Transaction Management Software Features to Consider

- File Audit
- Compliance Tracking
- e-Signature
- Document Sharing
- Form Integration
- Document Storage
- Contract Workflows
- Mobile App
- Integration
    - MLS
    - Email
    - CRM

- Financial Software

Best Transaction Management Software Options for Brokerages:

SkySlope

SKYSLOPE

Pricing: $7 per month per agent
Ease of use: Moderate

Ease of use and the ability to integrate with both the MLS and your financial management software make SkySlope a real estate transaction management software leader.

Dotloop

dot loop

Pricing: Contact for brokerage pricing
Ease of use: Moderate

Dotloop offers a very similar platform to Skyslope, so make sure to call both to get the best pricing for your brokerage.

Form Simplicity

Form Simplicity

Pricing: Contact for pricing
Ease of use: Easy

Form Simplicity is owned by the Florida Association of REALTORS but is available to agents and brokers nationwide. Form Simplicity offers fillable PDFs and agent transaction management, and broker compliance review, all from an easy-to-use interface.

Paperless Contracts & eSignature Software

Gone are the days of NCR paper, today real estate contract software is a must for any professional real estate agent. As a real estate broker, you may wish to provide your agents with real estate contract software. It will not only help you maintain standards, but it will also make your agents more efficient.

Many Board of REALTORs support a specific paperless contract software, and in some cities, it has become customary for agents to use the same software for ease of use. If your area or Board doesn't support a paperless contract solution, you may want to provide one for your agents.

Real Estate Paperless Contract & eSignature Software Features to Consider

- Interactive Contracts
- Web Signatures
- PDF Conversion
- Sign PDF Documents
- Client Access
- Calendar
- Deadline Monitor
- Branded Contracts
- Custom Clauses and Addendum
- Mac and PC
- Mobile Friendly
- File Backup
- Integrations
    - Calendar

- Email
- MLS
- Transaction Management

Best Paperless Contract & eSignature Software Options for Brokerages: 2021

DocuSign
Pricing: Start at $10 per agent
Ease of use: Easy

DocuSign is an end-to-end cloud-based paperless contract software solution. While the app is excellent consumer-facing I personally like the ability to communicate and share documents in the DocuSign Digital Rooms.

DocuSign is also one of the first companies to integrate blockchain technology onto its platform. That makes them an early mover into the consumer-facing blockchain smart contracts space. This is a technology that will revolutionize the real estate industry since contracts can be created and signed instantly with no intermediary.

Agent Recruiting Software

If you are going to dominate your market with your new real estate brokerage, you will need to recruit producing agents. Identifying the right agents by production and getting the correct contact information isn't as easy as it sounds. This is where robust recruiting software comes in.

Once you have identified your target agents, a CRM with proven email templates and the ability to text and drop voicemails will quickly become your best friend.

Agent Recruiting Software Features to Consider

- Email
- Voicemail Drop
- SMS Texting
- CRM
- Recruiting Campaign Templates
- MLS Agent Production Reports
- Data Import
- Automated Social Media Profile Lookup
- Training and Coaching
- Integration
  - Broker Metrics
  - Market View
  - MLS
  - Email
  - Calendar
  - Lead Forms
  - API

Best Agent Recruiting Software Options for Brokerages:

Brokerkit

Brokerkit

Pricing: Contact for pricing
Ease of use: Easy

Brokerkit combines a powerful CRM with email templates and integrates (SMS) texting directly from the system. This allows you to quickly contact more agents, build relationships faster, and recruit more agents.

SeizeTheMarket

SEIZE the MARKET

Pricing: $299 per month for two users
Ease of use: Easy

Seize the Market is a complete recruiting solution. With built-in marketing plans, agent production data, and delegated recruiting tasks, it would be difficult not to reach your brokerage agent goals.

BrokerMetrics

BrokerMetrics
AgentMetrics

Pricing: Contact for pricing
Ease of use: Easy

BrokerMetrics is not recruiting software but an MLS data provider that allows you to quickly analyze and download the necessary agent data from your MLS. You can quickly view agent production, company comparison, and contact information. An MLS subscription is required.

The Bottom Line

For those who are ready to jump into the competitive game of real estate brokerage, you must be prepared to win. To win at your brokerage, you must recruit and support your agents by providing them the necessary tools to succeed. The best way to do this is to have the right real estate broker software that supports the type of brokerage you are building.

Another common mistake new broker-owners make is hiring staff instead of using software or outsourcing to fulfill the agent's needs. This is a costly mistake. When your brokerage is small, hiring is the most expensive way to provide services. Therefore, when providing services and other agent resources you always want to start with software first, then outsource to a third party. Once your brokerage is large enough to afford staff you can hire to fulfill the tasks.

Take the time now to review the available real estate software options and pick the best software solutions for your brokerage. The time you spend here will save you tens of thousands of dollars later.

7

ARE OFFICES STILL NEEDED?

Reflecting on my 27-year career in real estate, I have seen many changes to real estate brokerages. Most of the changes have been in the use of technology to serve more agents, but the pandemic of 2020 may have forever changed the way real estate brokerages use brick-and-mortar office space.

So the question is: Will real estate brokerages even need brick-and-mortar offices in the future? In this chapter, I'll go over the pros and cons of brick & mortar offices, plus alternatives like co-working spaces and virtual brokerages.

Office Use Has Already Been on a Decline

In the early 2000s customers no longer needed to come to the office to sign contracts, thanks to home computers, printers, and the fax machine. Even before the pandemic, with high-speed internet, low-cost printers, and e-signatures, real estate agents mostly work from home and come to the brokerage office far less frequently.

When I had my real estate brokerage, to fill my empty private offices I tried to incentivize agents by offering them reduced fees if they worked from the office. I asked one top producer why he doesn't spend more time in the office, and he replied, *"Nobody here is going to buy or sell a house with me, and I can do my work from a coffee shop and actually meet potential buyers and sellers."* It is hard to argue with logic when you agree with it.

My experience of owning and coaching real estate brokerages has shown me that only between 10-20% of the agents (depending on the tenure of the agents) actually use a private or shared office. The remainder of the agents work remotely or from home, and this trend is likely to continue. Therefore, many brokerages went to an "open floor plan" concept that provides comfortable spaces for agents to drop into and a "hot desk" setup where agents do not even have a dedicated desk space to work.

The question now is, has the massive increase in working from home because of the pandemic further changed that trend, and if so, is it likely to stay that way?

The Pandemic Has Forever Changed the Brokerage Model

While working from the brick-and-mortar office was already on a decline, in my brokerage, we tried offering our team meetings and classes virtually. We thought that many of the agents would appreciate being able to participate from home using Zoom. What we found was that some seasoned real estate agents had little motivation to adapt to the technology needed to work remotely.

While the idea wasn't necessarily ahead of its time, many of the agents still struggled to understand how to use Zoom. Teaching them how to download the app and login was the first obstacle, but it was the pure lack of "Zoom Etiquette" (like dogs barking and an unknowing agent on camera in her unmentionables) that ultimately killed the idea.

Today the pandemic and lockdowns have forced brokerages and agents alike to learn and adapt to the technology to work and interact remotely. Even the most unwilling and technophobic are now able to log onto Zoom and participate in online classes and team meetings. Some agents have even found creative ways to provide virtual showings and open houses in areas with strict lockdown restrictions.

So this leaves the question… What exactly do we need the brick-and-mortar brokerage office for now? If I decided to start a new brokerage today, would I even bother with the expense and hassle of renting an office, or would I jump right to a virtual brokerage?

Are Virtual Brokerages the Solution?

A virtual, or "cloud-based," brokerage is one without a local, physical brokerage office. Many of the larger cloud-based brokerages like eXp Realty have proprietary software solutions that allow agents to virtually talk to the support staff for things like technical support, commission disbursement agreements, and even meet with their managing broker.

Prior to the pandemic, the idea of talking to your managing broker or having your team meeting virtually seemed more like a novelty than reality. Today, nearly every brokerage and agent has adapted to this new reality. Therefore, it seems now more than ever virtual brokerages are the way of the future.

The Benefits of a Virtual Brokerage

Potentially Lower Startup Costs
To the novice, it would seem that a virtual brokerage would cost much less to start than a traditional brick-and-mortar brokerage. Still, anyone who has invested in buying or creating proprietary software knows that software development can cost millions of dollars. eXp paid $11 million to purchase their proprietary software Virbella.

That being said, it is possible to start and operate a virtual brokerage with over-the-counter software like Lonewolf for the commission and financial management, Slack for team communication, and Zoom for meetings and training. This, combined with the fact that you won't be spending tens of thousands of dollars on leasing and setting up an office, can save you money over a brick-and-mortar startup.

Quicker Expansion & Easier to Scale
One of the most significant challenges with a brick-and-mortar brokerage is the risk and cost of expansion. When I had my brokerage, we expanded into four different markets. The cost to do this exceeded $600,000. Even with our large investment and good

intentions, one of our offices quickly failed, resulting in a loss of over $100,000.

Virtual brokerages don't have these risks. Since they are cloud-based and all agents access their brokerage services through the internet, your brokerage can quickly expand into other markets and even small sub-markets where larger traditional brokerages tend to overlook.

Tech-Savvy Agents

By necessity or by design, a virtual brokerage is more likely to attract independent, experienced, and tech-savvy agents. New and newer agents that need a lot of handholding will likely struggle in this environment, and the less technical will completely avoid it.

Type of Agents

More seasoned agents are more likely to want a brick-and-mortar office simply because of habit. In the first brokerage I worked at they required you to rent an office space. It was the belief at the time that agents with office space were more productive than agents without. Therefore, many of us more seasoned agents are accustomed to having an office to work from.

Additionally many small to mid-sized teams prefer the brokerage to provide office space since they are often too large to work from home and too small to afford their own office or co-working space.

Lower Operating Costs

Once your overall startup investment is made in the cloud-based infrastructure, the operational costs or cost/agent of running a virtual brokerage should (theoretically) be lower than operating a brick-and-mortar brokerage. This is simply because you are saving tens of thousands of dollars a year that you would typically be spending on rent.

Better Splits and Fees to Agents

The cost savings over the brick-and-mortar brokerage won't necessarily go directly into your pocket. Much, if not all, of these savings, will likely be passed onto the agents in the form of lower splits and fees than your traditional brokerage competitors.

Lower splits and fees do two things: On the positive, it can attract top producing agents and teams with their own staff and offices looking for lower brokerage expenses. On the negative side, lower fees also attract part-time and low-producing agents just looking to save money on the 1-2 transactions they do each year. You will want to keep this in mind when determining the type of agent you wish to attract to your brokerage.

Don't break out your *Programming for Dummies* book and start a virtual brokerage just yet though! Before you make this important decision, you must weigh it against the benefits of a brick-and-mortar office.

So, Are Brick-and-Mortar Offices Still Needed?

Before you tear up your office lease and go 100% virtual, there may be some reasons to keep your brick-and-mortar office. Remember the old saying, *"Before you take down a fence, know why it was built."*

There were many reasons why you needed an office in the first place, and some of those reasons haven't changed. Here are seven reasons why you might want a brick & mortar office that you might not have thought of:

7 Reasons for a Brick-and-Mortar Real Estate Office

1. **State Requirements**
   Some states require you to have a physical address for your brokerage. In some states, your home address may be sufficient to meet the requirements, and other states may require a location suitable for business operations.

2. **New Agent Training**
   If your brokerage has or plans to have new agents, then you probably want an office to train them in. It's no secret that

new agents need more attention than seasoned professionals. An office allows them a comfortable place for them to come to ask questions, take classes, and build good lead generation habits.

3. Private and Shared Offices

Although the trend has been leaning towards most agents working from home, many may still want to go to an office. Some agents feel more productive if they get out of the house to go to work, and others may not have the ability to work from home due to small children or other distractions, and some like to socialize. This creates an opportunity for brokerages that wish to still cater to agents that want or need a private or shared office to go to each day.

4. Brokerage Culture

The culture of your brokerage probably isn't the main reason agents will join your brokerage, but it is the main reason they will choose to stay. Culture is a real-world demonstration of the Mission, Vision, and Values of your brokerage. It is challenging to build a culture in the absence of social interactions. An office provides opportunities for social interactions, both planned and spontaneous.

While it isn't impossible to do this without a brick-and-mortar office, it is much more challenging. Camaraderie is essential for salespeople. While apps like Slack make this somewhat more manageable, the older agents who will likely be your top producers generally prefer in-person communication. It's hard to share a laugh with a colleague after a tough cold call on Slack.

5. Services

The typical services a real estate brokerage provides are not limited to broker supervision and file management. Many brokerages also offer agent marketing, listing marketing, transaction coordination, and printing and presentation services.

Today many brokerage administration services are easily managed either virtually or online. But anyone who has had to stand in line at Office Depot's Print & Copy Services departments knows that the ability to quickly create printable marketing and custom presentations without the support of someone who has a vested interest in your success is beyond frustrating.

Like many brokerages, one of my brokerage's most essential services was to help our agents to look and feel professional, and the printing and marketing pieces are a big part of that. A brick-and-mortar office provides a convenient place where your agents can have quick access to the equipment, services, and professional staff that will help them look top-notch.

6. Branding

An office can be much more than a place to print fliers and catch up on the latest industry news or gossip around the water cooler. A well-placed office with visible signage can help build brand awareness in your area. It can also show your customers and agents alike your commitment to the community and the vision of your brokerage. Let's face it, if you are willing to invest your hard-earned money into a long-term lease and the fixtures, finishes, and equipment of your office, you're likely committed to being around a long time.

7. Image

Call it ego; call it pride. There is something about walking into a professional office surrounded by Porsche Cayennes and BMWs. I always used to meet customers at my office because we had a beautiful office. I wanted them to see it! I can't speak for you, but I FEEL more successful, professional, and productive in a professional-looking office.

Of course, signing a multi-year lease on a flashy office isn't all wine and roses. There are two things you must consider before jumping into a brick-and-mortar office. The first is the significant upfront cost of tenant finishes, furniture, and equipment, and the second is committing a long-term lease. But, what if there was another option between a brick-and-mortar office and completely virtual, that doesn't require you to take all the financial risk? Well, there is… it's called a co-working space.

Is Co-Working Space the Best Option for Your New Brokerage?
Co-working space is typically high-end professional office space that is shared with multiple companies and other independent contractors.

If your brokerage is fewer than 20 agents, co-working space may be the right solution. This is because smaller brokerages usually have less need for office space. This is because they are generally too small to have multiple full-time staff, a new agent training schedule, or more than one or two agents who need private offices.

The challenge with co-working space is when your brokerage is larger than 20 agents or if the value proposition of your brokerage is a full-service marketing team. A co-working space requires you to share common areas like the kitchen, presentation rooms, and conference rooms with other individuals and companies. This can lead to scheduling conflicts for your in-person training classes and team meetings.

The other issue is the overall cost. If your brokerage is small, a co-working space can save you money. Yet the larger your brokerage gets, the more costly the co-working space becomes. Most co-working spaces include the utilities, internet, and cleaning into the lease rate. The lease rates range from $80-$120 per square foot, plus there are typically additional costs for the use of the conference rooms and training rooms.

Whereas, in a traditional office, your lease rate is much lower, ranging from $20-$50 per square foot, plus the costs of utilities, internet, phones, cleaning, etc. Therefore, if you are only renting a small 8'x 6' office in a co-working space, you may only pay $400 a month, but as you grow and need more space for agents and staff, your monthly costs and additional fees can quickly exceed the cost of leasing your own brick-and-mortar brokerage office.

The Bottom Line

While the pandemic has undoubtedly disrupted the brick-and-mortar real estate office, it likely won't eliminate it completely. If you are like me, you enjoy the flexibility of working from home but miss the social aspects and focus that an office environment brings.

Most of us in real estate are social and enjoy spontaneous interactions with other agents and staff. This is the main reason why I believe real estate brokerages will still offer some type of brick-and-mortar offices in the future. Because social interactions create culture, and a strong culture equals agent retention. It's that simple!

Therefore, if I was starting a brokerage today I would still provide a small brick-and-mortar office while offering all services and meetings virtually… The best of both worlds!

8

OFFICE SELECTION 101

The office space you select is yet another decision that can make or break your brokerage. In the middle of the great recession from 2010-2013, my partners and I were buying real estate brokerages for pennies on the dollar. Brokerages that were once worth over $500,000 we were buying for less than $50,000. The main reason for this was the expensive commercial lease.

You see, prior to the recession, the previous owners were optimistic about the future of their brokerage and the real estate market. Therefore they leased large, beautiful offices at the top of the market, hoping to grow into it. Then, when the market shifted and agents left the business, the brokerages found themselves struggling to pay the bills.

Since the lease was tied to the old entity, we would set up a new entity and purchase the furniture, equipment, and the franchise license from the current entity and move it all to a less expensive location.

Due to the pending recession, the commercial space was cheaper, and we could negotiate 3-6 months of free rent. This allowed us to be profitable from day one.

From this experience, I have come to believe that the greatest risk you will take starting your real estate brokerage is selecting the right office space and negotiating the best lease.

How to Select the Right Office

I have either repositioned or opened over twenty brokerages. In each case I had to determine the right office space. What I have found is there are eight things you must take into consideration in order to select the right office for your real estate brokerage.

Here are the 8 things you must take into consideration to find the right real estate brokerage office.

1. Your Brokerage's Mission and Vision

Begin with the end in mind. You wouldn't tell a client to buy a home with the intention of them having to sell it and buy a new home in just a few short months, would you? Of course not, because the cost of them having to sell, buy, and move defeats the point of owning a home.

The same is true for leasing an office. The cost of moving, the deposit, tenant improvements (TI), furniture, equipment, and signage is too high to have planned obsolescence in the near future. Not to mention the message moving offices sends to the long-term customers your agents are nurturing.

To prevent moving too soon, you must think with the end in mind. This is why you must be clear about the Mission, Vision, and Values (MVV) for your brokerage before you set out to find the right office space.

Your brokerage's mission is the difference your brokerage wishes to make in your community, demographic, or industry, and the vision is the picture of what it looks like when your brokerage realizes the goal it wishes to achieve.

Unless you are building a virtual brokerage, you wouldn't want to sign a long-term lease for a 600-square foot office if your vision is to have over 50 agents in the next 24 months.

The mission and vision for your brokerage will guide all the following decisions you must make when selecting the optimal office to fit your brokerage.

2. The Type of Agents You Wish to Attract

Something many future broker-owners forget when launching their brokerages is that most real estate brokerages exist to support the agent and the agent's job is to serve and support the customers. The way I represented this concept in my brokerage was to say,

"The "agent" is our customer, and the "client" is the agent's customer."

Before selecting an office, you must consider the type of agent you wish to serve and what type of clients they are working with. It really is as simple as that. Your office will be a giant advertisement for agents to come join you whether you want it to be or not.

Different agent types also have unique needs from their brokerage office. If your brokerage is designed to serve commercial real estate agents versus residential, you may need to have a downtown location to support the business clients in the area. If your ideal agents are working in a suburban area, then a downtown office location would be inconvenient for both the agents and their clients.

New, Newer, and Low-Producing Agents

As I've mentioned, full-time agents that produce less than 10 transactions a year typically need access to training and more one-on-one time than higher-producing agents. If your brokerage model is to have a large number of new or lower producing agents then plan on having or at least having access to a training room. This will allow you to manage a structured training schedule that won't interfere with the higher-producing agents.

Mid-Level to High-Producers

Agents that produce between 10-50 transactions a year are more likely to need access to marketing and transaction management support. Plan on about 20% of them also wanting to have a shared or private office to work from.

Top Producers and Teams

Top producers and teams need a larger private space to host their staff and licensed team members. This can be demanding for a small brokerage on a tight budget. The challenge that small brokerages face is providing the necessary office space and keeping their expenses within the budget.

3. The Services Your Brokerage Provides

Your real estate brokerage office's main function is to support the agent so they can serve their customers. Each brokerage model offers its agents different services depending on their value proposition. The more services you offer your agents, the more space you will need to support the staff to fulfill their needs.

If your brokerage's value proposition is to provide limited, à la carte services, or virtual services, then you may not need a lot of additional space for staff. On the other hand, if your brokerage's value is to offer one-on-one marketing support, you may need private offices for your staff, like a transaction manager and listing marketing coordinator.

4. The Location of The Office

Location, location, location, right? Well...maybe! Location is important but it may not be as important as some of the other considerations. I have seen very successful brokerages thrive in less-than-optimal office buildings.

There is no such thing as a "best location" for a real estate brokerage. What you are seeking is the best location that will fulfill your vision for your brokerage, that is right for the ideal agent types you wish to attract, and isn't too much of a burden on your budget.

Other Location Considerations

Of course, there are a few other things to keep in mind with your office location. These include:

Easy Access
Want to attract busy, producing agents? Then consider first-floor locations with abundant parking and easy access to highways. This will allow agents to quickly come and go in between appointments.

Local Amenities

An office that is near the amenities that make life generally better will not only attract agents but will increase their willingness to work from the office. This is because having the convenience of restaurants, coffee shops, gyms, and bike/walking trails will make coming to and working from the office a convenience not a hindrance.

Visibility and Signage
If your intention is for your location to attract walk-in customers you may want to consider locations in high-traffic areas. If you are wanting your location to promote your brand in a specific town or community, it helps to have either a location that is visible, like a corner location on the boardwalk or a Victorian home that everybody is familiar with. Don't overlook the benefits of a visible office or high-traffic location. In hot neighborhoods like Williamsburg in Brooklyn, a ground-floor retail office can see 20 or more walk-ins on a busy Saturday.

Office Location Within the Building
If your brokerage value is to provide more administrative services, competing on price, or there is little to no expectation for the majority of your agents to come into the office on a regular basis, then you may consider office locations that are less expensive.

The cost of office space greatly decreases as you increase to higher floors in an office building. Beware that top floors and breathtaking views can also demand a premium price. Another way to save on lease rates is to consider office buildings that are B- quality and lower. These are usually offices that are a little dated or not in ideal locations as it relates to ease of access.

I caution you to remember that to win at the real estate brokerage game you must be able to inspire the "right type of agents" to your brokerage that will also "want to affiliate" with your brokerage. Cutting corners when it comes to the location, visibility, access, or desirability of your office can result in the opposite effect.

I mean, what does a strip mall office with fluorescent lights and a drop ceiling say to potential new agents? Probably, that you place frugality above design, or that you don't spend a lot on agent support. Either way, is it how you want agents to perceive your brokerage?

It is easy to lose sight of this when you are looking at the available options for your brokerage. That being said, the most important factor is to stay within your budget.

5. Make a Budget and Stick to It

The #1 mistake I see broker-owners make is believing the myth **"If I build it, they will come."** While this is great for a movie plot, it is horrible advice for a real estate brokerage. This belief leads you to over-lease space that is either too large or too expensive for your current or short-term budget.

After the first three years of growing our modern boutique brokerage in Boulder, we felt that the 1400 square foot, Victorian-style house we were renting was holding us back from achieving our long-term goals.

In fact, at that time we had commitments from some top real estate agents and teams that if we were able to provide them high-quality office space that they would gladly join our brokerage. They literally said, "If you build it, we will come."

So, we decided it was time to upgrade our space and our image. My partners and I went out and scoped the available office space in Boulder. In the heat of a white hot commercial real estate market, we were finding office lease rates that ranged from $26-$55 a square foot. In addition to that, we wanted our own training room and open concept floor plan with ten private offices for both the staff and agents.

Our budget for this was $13,000 a month including utilities, taxes, parking, and maintenance. A good rule of thumb for how much of your budget to spend on your office space is to spend no more than 30% of your brokerage expense budget. The total lease cost should include any additional fees or expenses that may be charged or passed through to you by your landlord.

The risk of going above 30% of your expenses can result in you not having enough money left for day-to-day operations, innovations, and future opportunities. It's the equivalent of being house poor.

Additional Commercial Lease Expenses

If you're not familiar with commercial leases, beware there are additional expenses that you may be responsible for. Some commercial leases also charge Common Area Maintenance (CAM) or have additional expenses associated with the property that are passed through to you. These additional expenses include the following:

Office
Cleaning
Office Repairs and Maintenance
Water
Electricity
Gas
Internet
Property Insurance
General Liability Insurance
City Taxes
Building and Common Areas
Water
Electricity
Gas
Building Repairs and Maintenance

Property Taxes
Insurance
Security
Parking Repairs and Maintenance
Snow Removal
Landscaping
Trash

No matter what type of commercial lease agreement you are signing you must review the entire lease for these additional fees. Don't hesitate to ask for proof to show you what you can expect to pay in addition to your base rental rate.

6. The Size of the Office

The #1 reason new real estate brokerages struggle to be profitable or even ultimately fail is because they leased a space that is too large. Real estate offices are not like a traditional business; agents don't come in every day. In fact, your office will only be at full capacity when you are having a training event, team meeting, or social event. The rest of the time it will be at 20% capacity.

The size of your office is determined by the number of agents you wish to support, the types of services your brokerage provides, and of course your budget. A good rule of thumb for the size of a real estate brokerage office today is 30 square feet per agent or 1500 square feet for 50 agents.

The "30 square foot rule" assumes that 80% of your agents will be working mobily or from home. It also requires you to be efficient with your space and allows you to stay within your budget.

With more agents working virtually than ever before you may consider starting your brokerage with less square footage than the 30 square feet per agent. You may have to find new and creative ways to layout your brokerage office's floor plan so you can accommodate more agents with less space.

7. The Floor Plan

Mid-Sized Real Estate Brokerage Office

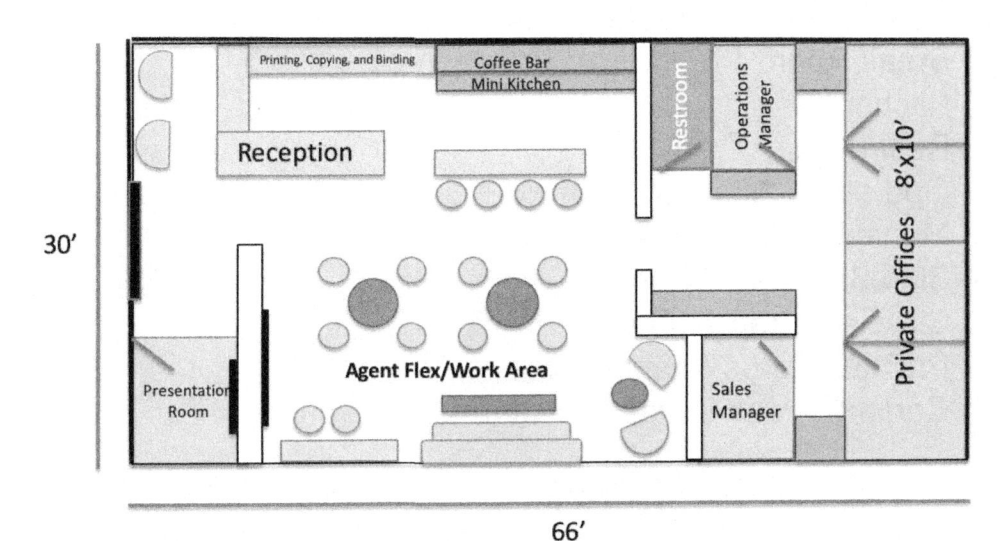

(Floor plan diagram: 30' x 66' = 2000 SQFT = 60 Agents. Includes Reception, Printing/Copying/Binding, Coffee Bar/Mini Kitchen, Restroom, Operations Manager, Private Offices 8'x10', Agent Flex/Work Area, Sales Manager, and Presentation Room.)

16 Strategies

Real estate brokerages have unique challenges when it comes to finding adequate floor plans. This is because, unlike most office workers, real estate agents don't come to the office 9-5 Monday through Friday. Additionally, traditional offices recommend 100-300 square feet per employee while real estate offices are closer to 30 square feet per agent.

Where a traditional business may have 6-10 employees in 2000 square feet you may have 60 agents plus staff in the same square footage. You need to be aware that this can cause issues when you have your training, team meetings, and social events. Issues like agents finding parking or a place to sit. You may even violate fire restrictions by exceeding the number of people allowed in a space.

Features to Consider for Your Brokerage's Floor Plan

- Reception Area
- Conference Room
- Agent Flex Work Area
- Training Room
- Print, Copy, and Binding Area
- Break Room
- Kitchen
- Restrooms
- Operations Manager's Office
- Managing Broker's Office
- Sign Storage
- Bicycle Storage
- Private/Shares Agent Offices
- Common Area Building Features

If the ideal office doesn't provide the right floor plan you can have the landlord make modifications or concessions in the lease so you can change or update the floor plan to meet your brokerage's needs.

8. The Terms of the Lease

The final consideration you must make is the terms of the lease. Sometimes you may find what seems like an ideal office, only to find that the lease terms are less than desirable. Before negotiating the lease for your new brokerage, know what terms you can live with and what terms you can't accept… And be willing to walk away!

Improvement Allowance

An Improvement Allowance is money that is provided by the landlord that is applied to the tenant's finishes to the office. This can include money for updating the offices, paint, carpet, kitchen, and even HVAC. Be aware though, this money is not free. It is baked into the lease rate and the term of the lease. Savvy landlords may also restrict what contractors are permitted to do repairs to the office.

This limits your ability to do updates "on the cheap" with your own contractors.

Lease Term

Avoid long lease terms that are longer than you expect to be in the property. If your brokerage is brand new you may want to start with a term of less than 2 years. Once you have established your brokerage an 8-10 year lease can lock in a low lease rate for the future.

Rent Increases

Some commercial leases will offer a very low or no rent for the first 6-months in order to get you in. Then later in the term of your lease the rental rate greatly increases beyond your ability to pay. It is easy when you are starting your brokerage to convince yourself that in a year or two your brokerage will be making money hand over fist.

Coming from experience, even if you are growing rapidly a sharp increase in your rent can wreck your profitability and send your brokerage into a tailspin. Select an office with a predictable lease rate and don't be overconfident with your projections.

Personal Guarantee

A Personal Guarantee is a clause that says if for some reason your brokerage doesn't have the ability to pay the rent or even fails completely, then the landlord can pursue the Guarantor (in this case you) for the lost rent plus any additional incurred expenses.

Avoid Personal Guarantees at all costs. Business is difficult enough, and they can fail for all kinds of reasons. Some are in your control and others are outside of your control. The last thing you need is the fear of a Personal Guarantee looming over your head.

Flexibility

Also, look for terms that give you some flexibility. Real estate is notoriously boom and bust. Therefore, real estate brokerage leases need more flexibility than a traditional business. If your real estate brokerage takes off you may need the ability to expand within the same building or sublease your space to another tenant so you can move to another location.

Early Termination

If your brokerage struggles or fails you may need the option to cancel the lease so you can move on without the fear of future lawsuits or bankruptcy. This can be done by negotiating an early termination fee into your lease. This is typically equal to 3-6 months of rent plus repayment of any improvement allowance and discounted rent.

Cautionary Tale: The Boulder Office

Like many broker-owners, I have previously fallen into the trap where my desires far exceeded my budget. When looking for our new Boulder office, we found a nice 3500 square foot office that offered everything we wanted and was within our budget. However, due to the fire code requiring two exits, we could not have a 20-person training room within the space.

The landlord saw this as an opportunity to quickly offer up an adjacent 1700 square foot office that could be converted into a training room. To help us fit it into our budget he offered to abate the additional rent for a few months until we could fill the office with all our new agent prospects and allow the additional space to fit within our budget.

My partners and I knew that believing the "build it and they will come" fallacy was bad logic. However, we thought we had the commitment from the top producing agents and the teams that said they would join us if we could provide them office space. We also believed our growth would continue at the same pace that it had been in the previous years.

Excited about the fancy new location and dreams of agents and teams filling the offices and training room, my partner and I agreed to the larger space. All-in the 5200 square foot office cost $17,000 a month including the NNN for the first 6- months then it began to escalate to over $23,000 a month over the next 7-years.

But this wasn't the worst part of the deal. Since our company was only 3-years old, the landlord required us to personally guarantee the full term of the lease. As residential real estate agents, neither my partner nor I had experience in negotiating commercial leases. With this, combined with our optimism about the future of our infant brokerage, we agree to sign the lease.

This will turn out to be the biggest mistake I've made in all my years in broker ownership. I will share in detail later. In the meantime, just note that if you haven't written and negotiated over 100 commercial leases, then hire an attorney or a commercial real estate professional who has. The success of your business and your future financial security depends on your ability to negotiate the right terms of your brokerage's lease.

The Bottom Line

Your lease may be the most important detail and the greatest financial risk you will take opening a new real estate brokerage. Take your time and look for the right opportunity that checks all the right boxes.

9

STAFFING UP FOR SUCCESS

Whether you open a small independent brokerage or you're running a large national franchise, each of the launches or relaunches require not only hiring employees at all levels of the brokerage but also firing employees who are not performing or where their roles are no longer needed. The key is understanding what staff you need at the right time or phase your brokerage is in. This is often based on the size of the brokerage and the services you choose to provide your agents.

I will share which employees you need to hire to successfully grow your real estate brokerage from a small brokerage with just one employee, to a large brokerage with a full staff.

Roles Are Not Employees

Before you start hiring for your brokerage, there is a simple rule of thumb you need to understand. You need to hire for roles, not employees. Roles are a title given that encompasses all of the responsibilities of an employee. Each employee can and likely will have one or more roles within your real estate brokerage, especially in the early stages of growth.

For example, you may choose to start your real estate brokerage with just one employee and yourself. If you do, then you must divide the roles required to run the brokerage between the two of you. As your brokerage grows and you hire new employees you will train and hand off each of the roles to the new employees.

There are ten essential roles to run a real estate brokerage. Each role has specific tasks called responsibilities. Below is a list of each of the roles and the corresponding responsibilities required to run a successful real estate brokerage.

10 Roles and Responsibilities for a Real Estate Brokerage

Role	Responsibilities
Office Manager	Financial management
Receptionist	Answer phones, greet guests, showing coordination, open and close office
Transaction Manager	File review and compliance
Marketing Manager	Create and prepare all marketing materials for agents and brokerage
Listing Manager	Coordinate and prepare properties for sale
Lead Manager	Coordinate and manage leads and follow-up
Managing Broker	Review file for legal compliance
Mentor	Mentor agents and lead training classes
Sales Manager	Recruit agents and lead sales team
Transaction Coordinator	Assists agents with managing dates and deadlines, signatures, and gathering required documentation

How Many Employees Do You Need to Start and Grow Your Real Estate Brokerage?

Figuring out how many employees you will need to run a successful real estate brokerage is not easy. Making the right hire and when to hire depends greatly on what real estate brokerage model you are running and what types of services you choose to offer your agents.

In an attempt to answer this question for you, I will make some assumptions. First, let's assume you are opening a full-service brokerage; you provide full listing assistance, agent marketing, transaction coordination, and maybe you provide some paid leads. In exchange for what you offer, the agents are on a 60/40 split plus an additional referral fee on brokerage leads. Lastly, let's assume your average agent is producing the NAR average of 1 transaction a month.

Let's take a look at how your brokerage will most likely grow over the next few years from this starting point, called The Incubation Phase, all the way to your goal, the Large Brokerage Phase. To help with your forecasting, each example below will include the employees necessary, the coordinating roles, and an estimated salary of each employee.

Incubation Phase (< 24 Agents)

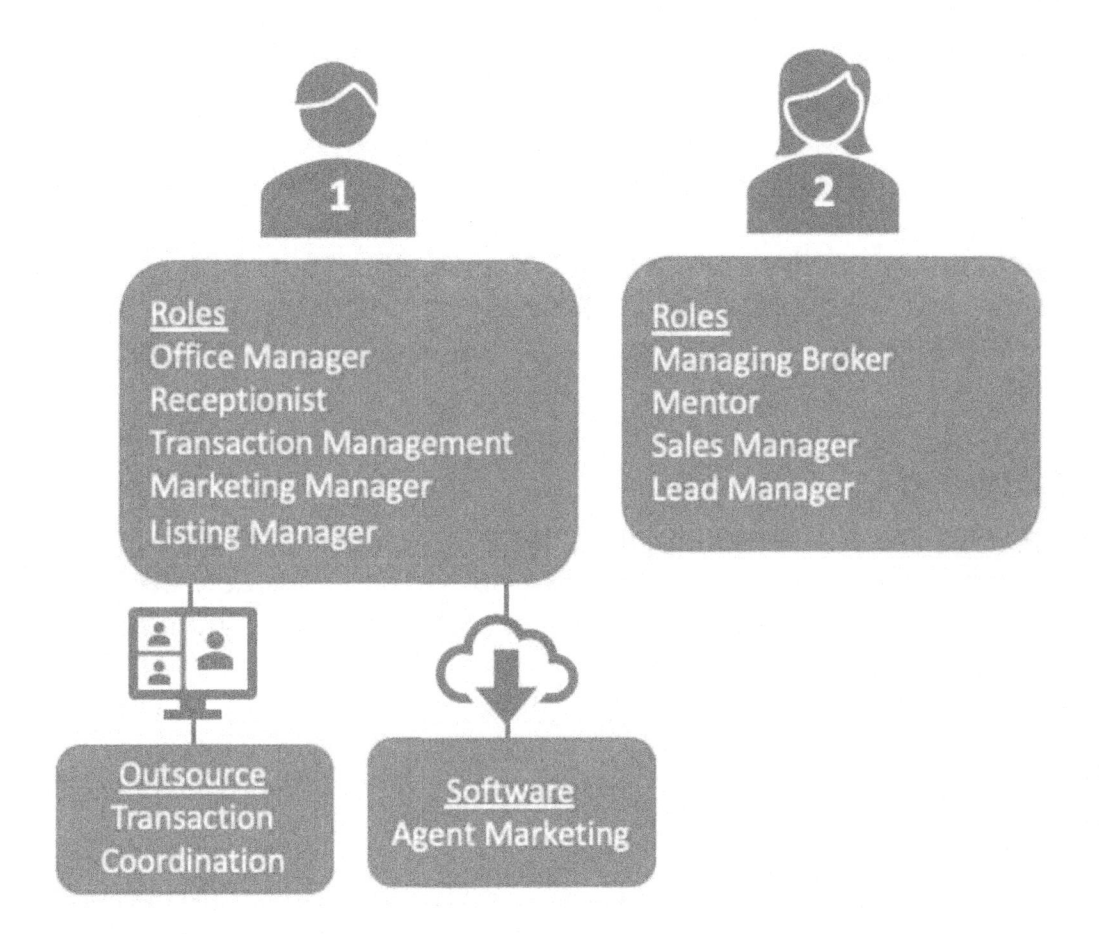

Incubation Phase

1

Roles
Office Manager
Receptionist
Transaction Management
Marketing Manager
Listing Manager

2

Roles
Managing Broker
Mentor
Sales Manager
Lead Manager

Outsource
Transaction Coordination

Software
Agent Marketing

In the Incubation Phase (less than 24 agents) your focus should be on sustainably growing your brokerage while keeping your eye on expenses. Many new brokerages never make it out of this phase due to mismanaging their expenses or underestimating the difficulty of recruiting. Either way, to keep costs low you will need to share all the roles and responsibilities required to manage a brokerage with only one full-time employee.

Here is a quick breakdown of how you might share roles with your first hire, an office manager:

Hire: Office Manager
Salary: $32,000-$65,000

When you are just starting you need to hire an employee that is a multitasker. Not because you are trying to take advantage or you can't hire a specialist, but because the size of your brokerage at this phase isn't going to produce enough revenue to hire multiple people. Therefore, they are going to have to handle multiple operational roles.

Depending on the number of transactions you are closing each month you will need either a part-time or full-time employee. The starting salary for this position will be between $32,000 to $65,000 a year.

DIY: Sales Manager
Salary: n/a

Since you're a licensed broker, have sales skills, and care about your brokerage more than anyone else, you will probably be the one responsible for the tasks of recruiting, mentoring, lead management, and Managing Broker duties. To keep costs low you may not take a salary in the beginning, but over time you can start paying yourself a reasonable salary.

Outsource: Transaction Coordination
Salary: $150-$300 per file

Consider outsourcing transaction coordination from the beginning. For one, it will save you and your Office Manager a lot of time not chasing agents for their paperwork, and secondly, if you charge your agents for transaction coordination, it may actually become a profit center for your brokerage, and thirdly, they may be able to manage your brokerage compliance file.

Today there are many outstanding transaction coordinators. Most are state-specific due to the local nuances and charge between $150-$300 a file depending on the volume you will be sending them.

Purchase: Agent Marketing Software

In this phase, you are going to need to be very resourceful, as it is not uncommon to be running your brokerage at a loss at this time. Software solutions like Breakthrough Broker (free version) or Lab Coat Agents Marketing Center ($59 / month) can help with managing your agents' marketing needs at little to no cost to you.

Incubating Brokerage Employee Roles and Salaries

Employees	Roles	Salaries
Employee 1 (Office Manager)	Office Manager, Receptionist, Transaction Manager, Listing Manager, Marketing Manager	Full-time $32,000-$65,000/Yr
Employee 2 (You)	Sales Manager, Managing Broker, Mentor, Lead Manager	$0-$40,000/Yr
Outsource	Transaction Coordinator	$150-$300/File
Total		$55,000-$125,000

Small Brokerage (25-39 Agents)

Small Brokerage

1
Roles
Office Manager
Receptionist
Transaction Management

2
Roles
Managing Broker
Mentor
Sales Manager
Lead Manager

3
Roles
Marketing Manager
Listing Manager

Outsource
Transaction Coordination

Software
Agent Marketing

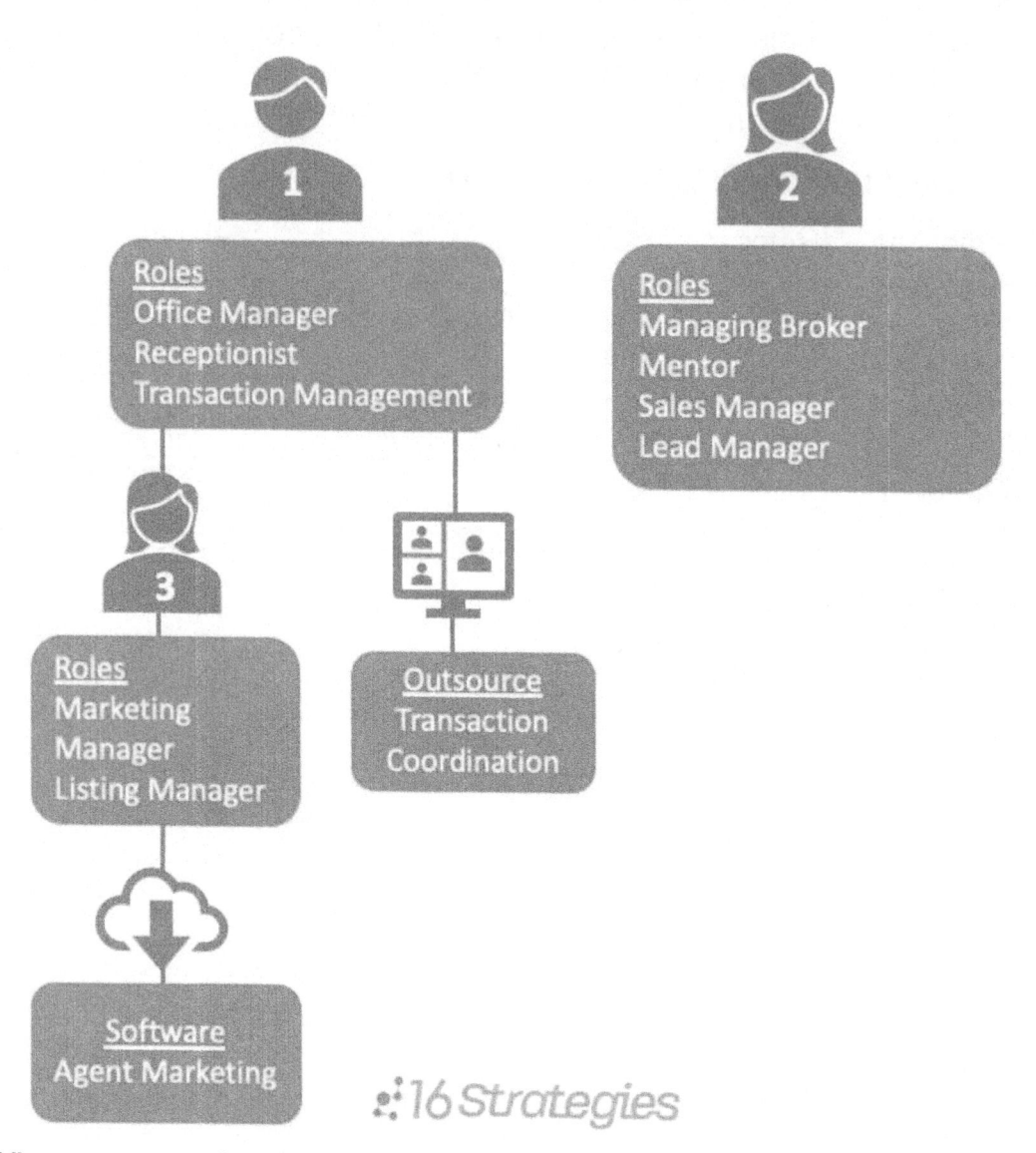

∴ 16 Strategies

When your real estate brokerage passes 25 agents and enters the "Small Brokerage Phase," hiring another employee is critical for growth. Ideally, at this point, your staff will be onboarding at least ten listings and closing over 25 transactions each month. This will become increasingly difficult for one person to manage on their own.

New Hire: Marketing and Listing Manager

When you hit the first milestone of 25 agents you need to be prepared to hire a third employee and separate Listing Management and Marketing Management tasks from the other operational duties of the brokerage.

Your third employee may be part-time at first, then move to a full-time position later. While the cost to hire this position depends on the experience of the employee, you can expect to pay at least $15-$20 an hour to find someone with the skills necessary to handle the responsibilities of both the Listing and Marketing Management Roles.

Find someone that is great with getting things done while keeping a smile on their face, as they will be working directly with your listing agents.

Small Brokerage Employee Roles and Salaries

Employees	Roles	Salaries
Employee 1 (Office Manager)	Office Manager, Receptionist, Transaction Manager	Full-time $45,000/Yr +
Employee 2 (You)	Sales Manager, Managing Broker, Mentor, Lead Manager	$0-$40,000/Yr + bonus
Employee 3 (Marketing and Listing Manager)	Listing Manager, Marketing Manager	Part-time or full-time $30,000- $45,000/Yr
Outsource	Transaction Coordinator	$150-$300/File
Total		$85,000-$165,000

Medium Brokerage (40-59 Agents)

Medium Brokerage

1
Roles
Office Manager
Receptionist
Transaction Management

2
Roles
Sales Manager
Lead Manager

3
Roles
Marketing Manager
Listing Manager

Outsource
Transaction Coordination

4
Roles
Managing Broker
Mentor

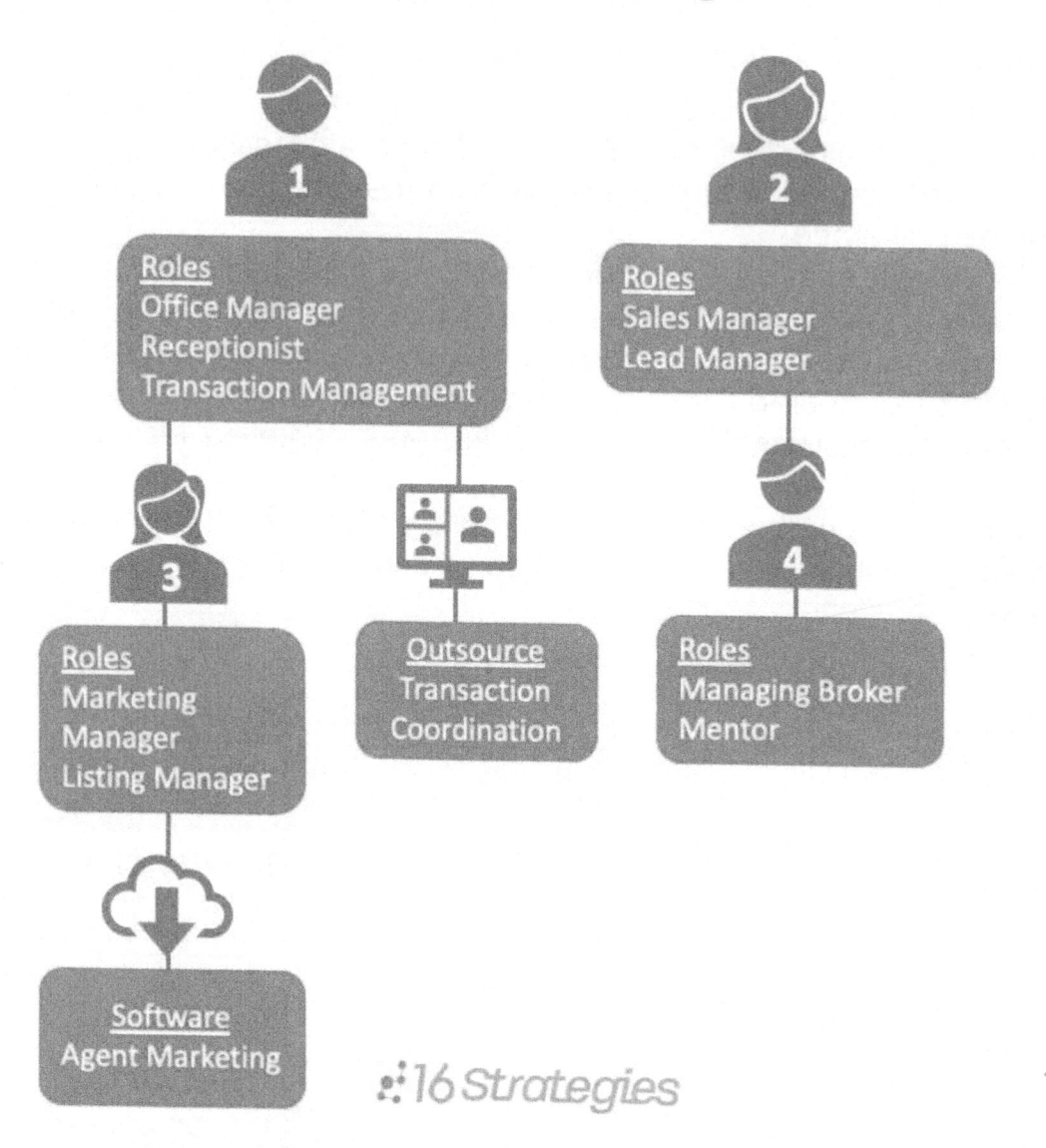

Software
Agent Marketing

16 Strategies

At 40+ agents, you reach the "Medium Brokerage" phase. Of course, as they say "mo money, mo problems." With success, comes the challenges of handling even more listings, agents, and closings. All while still recruiting, onboarding agents, and serving your agents. At this point, you, as the head of sales, are reaching your limit.

The good news is your brokerage should be productive enough to pay you a fair salary and hire someone to take some tasks off your busy plate.

Hire: Managing Broker/Mentor

At this stage of growth, you need help mentoring the newer agents and handling the Managing Broker duties. You may believe as the owner of a real estate brokerage hiring someone else to be the Managing Broker and Mentor to the agents may seem like a mistake.

Remember, as the owner of your real estate brokerage, your number one responsibility is to attract new recruits and lead the agents within your brokerage. Hiring someone to handle the day-to-day new agent questions and review the contracts will keep your head clear and your time free to focus on growing your brokerage's productivity.

Pro tip: Hire from Within When Possible

An experienced agent in your brokerage may make an ideal Managing Broker. The compensation can start at $40,000/Yr or they may be willing to handle the Managing Broker responsibilities for a free or reduced CAP or reduced fees. The compensation for mentoring can be structured as 50% of the additional split that a new agent pays in exchange for the additional supervision and training.

Medium Brokerage Employee Roles and Salaries

Employees	Roles	Salaries
Employee 1 (Office Manager)	Office Manager, Receptionist, Transaction Manager	Full-time $45,000/Yr +
Employee 2 (You)	Sales Manager, Lead Manager	$60,000/Yr + bonus
Employee 3 (Marketing	Listing Manager, Marketing	Part-time or full-time

and Listing Manager)	Manager	$30,000- $45,000/Yr
Employee 4 (Managing Broker)	Managing Broker, Mentor	Full-time $40,000/Yr +
Outsource	Transaction Coordinator	$150-$300/File
Total		**$145,000-$265,000**

Large Brokerage (60 Agents or More)

Large Brokerage

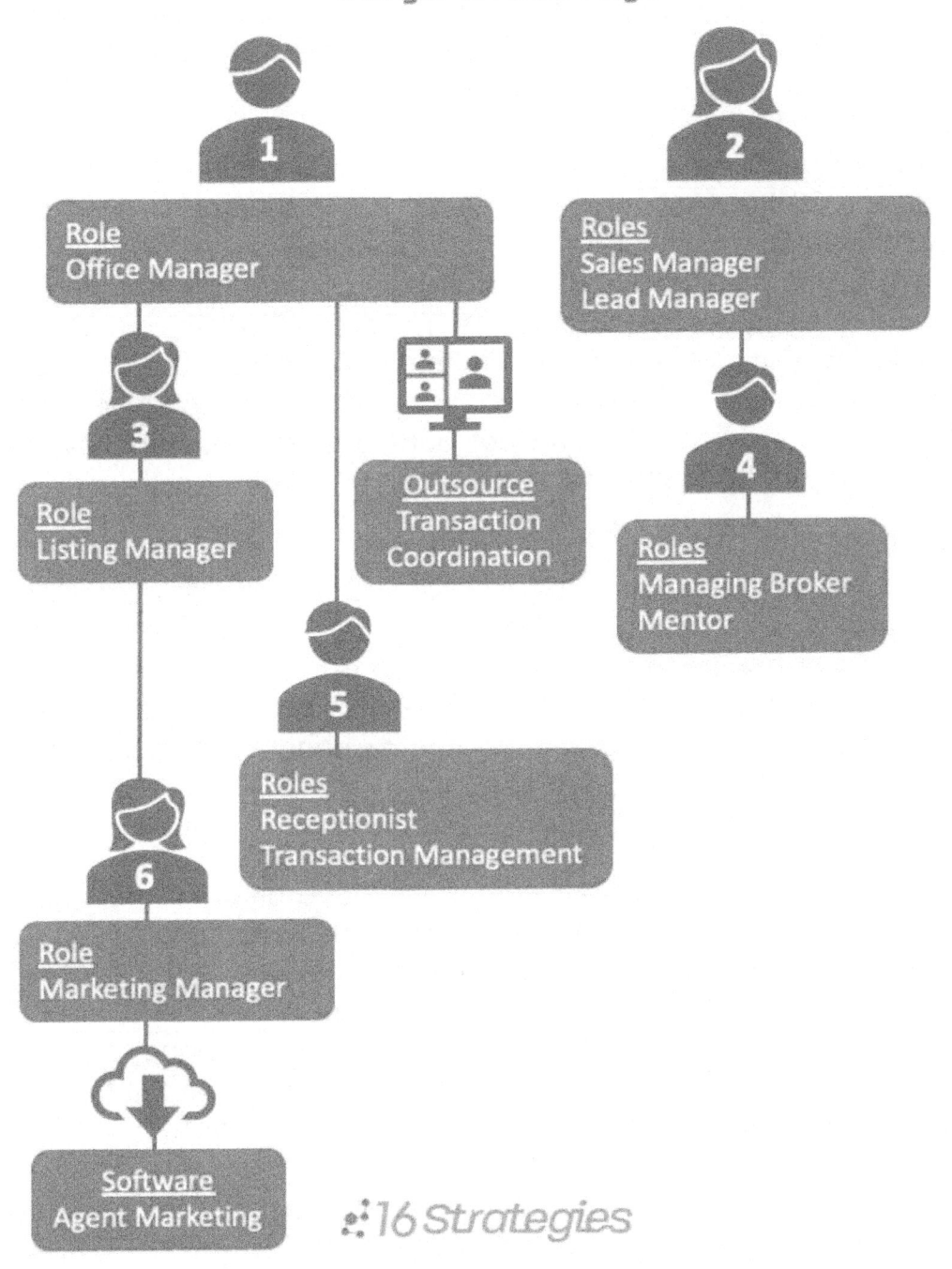

1
Role: Office Manager

2
Roles: Sales Manager, Lead Manager

3
Role: Listing Manager

4
Roles: Managing Broker, Mentor

5
Roles: Receptionist, Transaction Management

6
Role: Marketing Manager

Outsource: Transaction Coordination

Software: Agent Marketing

∴ 16 Strategies

When you reach the tipping point of 60+ agents your "Large Brokerage" is well on its way to becoming a respected brand in your community. Don't run out and buy an Escalade wrapped with your logos yet! This is your opportunity to 10X your brokerage...or burn your staff out if you don't follow my advice.

Your 60+ agents on a slow month are now onboarding 10+ listings and closing 30 transactions each month, but in the spring they can easily bring in 50 listings and over 80 closings in a single month.

Sure your hard-working and talented staff could easily handle the transactions if they came in consistently throughout the year, but your staff may get overwhelmed in the busy months if you don't prepare by staffing up for the busy seasons. To continue your growth, serve your agents, and not burn out your key employees you need to staff up to the next level.

Hire: Receptionist/Transaction Manager

The next hire is to provide some relief to your Office Manager. Start with a part-time receptionist to answer phones, greet agents and guests, and to handle the day-to-day office operations. The starting salary for this position is around $15-$20 an hour. If you see the need, bring the receptionist on full-time to handle the receptionist duties and Transaction Management.

Hire: Marketing Manager

As your brokerage grows your agents will have different marketing needs. Managing these marketing needs can become challenging for a full-service brokerage. If you wish to retain your top producing agents and teams you will need to give them access to a highly-skilled graphic design professional. Start with someone working part-time and if you see there is demand bring them on full-time. A highly skilled graphic design person can easily start at $60 an hour and go higher.

The responsibilities of the Marketing Manager can also be outsourced to a qualified graphic design person. The risk is that an outsourced person is not an employee so it is difficult to hold them accountable for strict deadlines.

Large Brokerage Employee Roles and Salaries

Employees	Roles	Salaries
Employee 1 (Office Manager)	Office Manager	Full-time $50,000/Yr +
Employee 2 (You)	Sales Manager, Lead Manager	$60,000/Yr + bonus
Employee 3 (Listing Manager)	Listing Manager	Part-time or full-time $30,000-$45,000/Yr +
Employee 4 (Managing Broker)	Managing Broker, Mentor	Full-time $40,000/Yr +
Employee 5 (Receptionist)	Receptionist, Transaction Manager	Part-time or full-time $30,000-$45,000/Yr +
Employee 6 or Outsource (Marketing Manager)	Marketing Manager	Part-time or full-time $20,000-$60,000/Yr +
Outsource	Transaction Coordinator	$150-$300/File
Total		$235,000-$395,000

The Bottom Line

There are many factors that will ultimately determine how many employees your brokerage will need, and when you will need to hire them. Some of these factors are your agent compensation model, your budget, and if your brokerage is in a brick-and-mortar office or virtual environment.

In any case, keep your expenses low at first by utilizing software to handle as many tasks as possible. Use outsourcing for things like creating marketing materials before hiring full-time employees.

    Lastly, be prepared by having a clear plan to hire long before you need the employee. This will give you time to budget, hire, and train your next employee before you are rushed to fill the role with just anyone.

10

IDENTIFY BROKERAGE OPERATIONS AND PROCEDURES

There are many benefits to having a procedures manual for your real estate brokerage. Written procedures will systematize your brokerage saving time and allowing for quicker growth.

In a real estate brokerage, there are no simple decisions or tasks. Even basic tasks like making coffee are important enough to create a procedures plan. You might not think something as trivial as making coffee can hurt your business, but small failures add up and can ripple out to become big failures.

Imagine a receptionist that is in charge of buying coffee, without having a procedures manual, may buy their favorite organic Ethiopian coffee, because they like the taste. Later you hear that many of the agents say it tastes too strong. So you address it with the employee and ask them to buy a milder name brand.

Problem solved, right? Wrong. When you hire a new receptionist and they don't know about the "Coffee Wars" of just a few months ago, and in an attempt to save some money they buy the cheapest coffee. Starting "Coffee War II." This all could have been solved if you had a simple written procedures manual for the new employee to follow.

Your procedures manual will also set standards and define objectives. This leads to a better experience for both the agents and their clients. I will share with you a full list of the procedures to operate a real estate brokerage, show you how to create your own procedures, and help you create your procedures manual.

Example Procedures List

Like the employee organizational chart from the previous chapter. I have broken the tasks into two categories: Sales and Operations.

Sales Procedures

These are all the tasks that are the responsibility of the employees that support the sales side of the brokerage.

CATEGORY	PROCESSES AND PROCEDURES	FREQUENCY	RESPONSIBLE
Agent Support			
	Communications Schedule	Bi-Weekly	Sales Manager
	Team Meeting Schedule	Weekly	Sales Manager
	Continuing Education Schedule	Quarterly	Sales Manager
Agent Recruiting			
	Agent Recruiting Plan	Weekly	Sales Manager
	Agent Onboarding Plan	Weekly	Office Manager
	Agent Off-Boarding Plan	Weekly	Office Manager
Lead Management			
	Advertising Plan and Budget	Monthly	Lead Manager
	Lead Management Plan	Weekly	Lead Manager
	Agent Accountability	Weekly	Sales Manager
Brokerage Marketing Plan			
	Community Involvement	Monthly	Sales Manager
	Advertising Plan and Schedule	Monthly	Sales Manager
New Agent Training			
	Pre-License Education	Quarterly	Mentor

| | Structured New Agent Training Plan | Quarterly | Mentor |

Operations Process and Procedures

These are all the tasks that are the responsibility of the employees that support the operations side of the brokerage.

CATEGORY	PROCESSES AND PROCEDURES	FREQUENCY	RESPONSIBLE
Office Management			
	Agent Split/Fee Management	Monthly	Office Manager
	Commission Disbursement Process	Weekly	Office Manager
	Agent Billing Process	Monthly	Office Manager
	Escrow Accounts Management	Daily	Office Manager
	Financial Review and Management	Monthly	Owner
	Employee Hiring and HR Management	Weekly	Office Manager
	Annual Tax Filing Plan	Annually	Office Manager
Agent/Listing Marketing			
	Agent Marketing Support Plan	Monthly	Marketing Manager
	Listing Marketing Plan	Daily	Listing Manager
Office Maintenance			
	Coffee and Supplies	Weekly	Receptionist
	Printing and Copy	Weekly	Receptionist
	Cleaning and Repairs	Weekly	Receptionist

	Landscaping and Snow Removal	Seasonally	Receptionist
	Security	Daily	Receptionist
	IT Support	As Needed	Receptionist
Agent Supervision			
	File Compliance Process	Daily	Transaction Manager
	Broker Contract Review Plan	Daily	Managing Broker
	Industry Changes and Updates Communications Plan	Monthly	Managing Broker
	Broker Question Process	Daily	Managing Broker

How to Create Procedure Plans for Your Real Estate Brokerage

It may sound like overkill, but in the long run, using a procedures plan at every level of your brokerage will save you a lot of time and headache. A procedures plan requires more than a simple description of the task. There are six features to each procedure plan.

6 Features of a Procedure Plan:

1. Objective
   What's the desired outcome of this task? Clear and measurable objectives are best. This ensures that everyone knows what is expected from them.

   Example
   The sales manager's objective is to recruit two agents a month to grow the brokerage and keep it profitable.

2. Who

Who's responsible for completing the task? The person responsible for completing the task is not necessarily the person who actually does the work. For instance, the receptionist may be responsible for the office looking clean and tidy although they are not the one actually cleaning the office after hours.

This is someone who you can hold accountable for success or failure for the task, as well as the point person that agents and other employees can look to for support or answers.

3. How

    How's the task to be completed? This is a detailed step-by-step explanation of how to complete each task. This ensures that the employee that is given the task can follow with little or no additional supervision.

4. Frequency

    How often does this task need to be completed? Some tasks are daily, some weekly, some monthly, and some are annual. To ensure that tasks are not forgotten, each employee must have a clear understanding of when and how often the tasks are to be completed.

5. Standards

    What are the quality standards for the task and how are they measured? Each task has a measure of the standard that must be followed. Even a task as simple as answering the phone must have clear standards. You don't want your receptionist answering the phone with "What's up, dude?" Do you?

6. Budget

    What's the budget for the task? If the task requires the employee to spend money, how much can they spend without asking for approval? Whose permission do they need to go over this budget?

Procedures Plan Template for Real Estate Brokerages

If you are serious about starting a real estate brokerage, the time to start writing out your procedures is now. To get started by downloading my free Procedures Plan Template at https://theclose.com/brokerage-resources

The Procedures Manual is Your Playbook

Before I go too deep into this analogy, I wish to disclose that I am not a big sports guy. So if my descriptions sound uninformed it is because I am. Nevertheless, we will continue.

A football coach doesn't wait for the season to begin to start writing plays, and as far as I know, successful coaches don't make up plays in the middle of a game either… And neither should you!

If you wait to start your brokerage before you begin your procedures manual, you will essentially be trying to write your plays during the game. The reason this leads to failure is because during the game you are not thinking with a long-term or big picture mindset.

When you are in the middle of the week, I call this "Game Time", you are focused on supporting your agents by training them or servicing their needs. You are likely focused on quickly putting out fires, and like a firefighter the quicker you put out a fire the less damage they can cause.

For example, imagine you were faced with a situation where a top producing agent, we'll call her Rosemary, asked your Office Manager, we'll call him James, to help her input her three new listings into the MLS. The rule in the office is to have the agents input their own listing so this request was not expected by James.

James responded that it isn't something he can do since it wasn't the responsibility of the brokerage. Additionally, he was already busy with his own workload.

As a broker-owner, you don't want to upset James and you certainly don't want to offend Rosemary. Thinking this is a one-time occurrence, you offer to input the listings yourself. That evening you stay late and input the three listings for Rosemary.

The following Monday at your Operations Meeting, James is upset with you because you made the decision to input the listings for Rosemary. His concern is that she will now have the expectation that this is something that the brokerage will provide in the future. He continues to point out that you don't have the time to input listings and manage your busy schedule.

You quickly realize that James is correct, and you "Wrote a Play" during "Game Time." You also see that this was a short-term solution that will lead to long-term consequences or expectations.

To prevent this, you need to avoid making decisions during Game Time and move all your decisions about agent services, process changes, and additions or subtractions to employee roles to your Operations Meeting.

Like a football coach that reviews the game tape at the end of the week, you too can review all agent requests, employee concerns, and upcoming decisions outside of the day-to-day operations of your brokerage. You can do this by setting aside 2-4 hours each week to review the decisions with a long-term mindset.

Once a decision is made, a procedure is written out, it is added to the Procedures Manual, and shared with the rest of the staff.

As for James and Rosemary, you can add an additional service for a small fee to have one of the seasoned agents in the brokerage input the listing for Rosemary or any other agents that needs this service.

This long-term solution can provide additional revenue for the brokerage and can be seen as a benefit to other busy agents that are shopping brokerages.

Create Your Procedures Manual

Now that you have created the list of procedures to run your real estate brokerage and have started the exhaustive process of detailing each task, you will need to keep each procedure plan accessible to you and your employees by creating a procedures manual.

Sure you can save it in a shared drive, but I have found that agents and employees will quickly forget that it exists. Keep your important procedures top-of-mind by printing the manual and bringing it to your meetings for reference.

Steps to Create Your Procedures Manual

1. Print and Bind

Print your procedures manual and keep it in a three-ring binder. This will allow you to easily update it and add to sections without having to re-print the entire manual.

2. Categorize it by Roles

Separate the procedure plans by the employee that is responsible for the completion of the task. This will allow the employees to have a quick reference to the procedures that they are responsible for.

3. Lead By Example

To rapidly grow your brokerage, you need the new employees to quickly pick up the tasks they are responsible for. You can lead by example by bringing the procedures manual to employee meetings and reference it often.

4. Keep it Up-To-Date

If changes are made to a task the person responsible for the task is also accountable for updating the procedures plan and procedures manual for that task. This ensures that procedures are being followed and that they are always up-to-date.

The Bottom Line

To build a brokerage that will support agents and rapid growth, you'll need to devote some time NOW to consider and define the procedures that are important and necessary to support your brokerage, agents, and your community.

11

SPLITS AND FEES TO ATTRACT THE RIGHT AGENTS

Over the years, I learned an important lesson about agent compensation: **How you pay your agents can be more important than how much you pay your agents.** Why? Because it doesn't matter what your splits and fees are if you have no agents.

When my partners and I envisioned our brokerage, we knew that we wanted to begin with supporting both newer and lower-producing agents. We believed if we could grow our newer agents into high and top producers, we would get the attention of the other agents in Boulder to want to check us out.

Knowing this, we would need an agent compensation model that would allow an agent's business to grow within our brokerage, and their splits and fees to be flexible so they won't leave once their business gets momentum.

This wasn't as easy as it sounds, and it only becomes more difficult when your agents become top producers. To help you decide on the right approach for you, I am going to go over the most common splits, monthly fees, and additional services that successful brokerages are using to attract top agents.

Then I'll discuss some ways to increase revenue with additional fees and go over some common mistakes new broker-owners make with compensation plans.

The Numbers Game: Transaction Fee Models

In part due to the advancements in cloud-based real estate software, the **transaction fee model** has exploded over the last few years. This model provides the basic real estate brokerage services for a very low monthly fee plus a "transaction fee" upon a successful sale. All other services such as marketing, training, E&O, etc. must be purchased separately by the agent.

Most transaction fee models have a monthly fee that ranges from $35 to $75 a month depending on the additional resources the brokerage offers. These resources may include lead generation websites, a CRM, or a central office.

The transaction fees that are due when a commission is earned run between $250 to $500. A very low amount compared to a split. Like a split to a cap model, in some cases these fees can cap for top producing agents that reach certain production milestones.

Is the Transaction Fee Model Right for Your Brokerage?

Although I have never worked for or owned a transaction fee model brokerage, I have coached broker-owners that have this brokerage model. I have come to see that this business model can be very profitable. That is… once you are over 200 agents!

Due to the low monthly fee and small commission share, the real challenge with this model is growing your agent count fast enough to get to the break-even point before you run out of working capital.

The way most transaction fee models have solved remaining profitable is by going completely virtual and requiring all the agents to work remotely. In the past, this has been a difficult sell to seasoned agents that are used to going to an office each day but Covid may have changed that perspective.

If you are starting a brick-and-mortar brokerage and you want less risk of losing money for months then consider the next compensation models.

Share the Wealth: Split Compensation Models

Even though this model has been losing ground to some of the other models, the **split commission model** is still the most common model in the real estate industry. This model started back in the 1950s when the real estate brokerage's role was to attract customers through their marketing and advertising. Then the agent's role was to serve the customers by listing or selling them a home. The commissions earned were then "split" between the brokerage and the agent.

Most split compensation models have a very low monthly fee with an agreement for the agent to pay a larger portion of their commissions to the brokerage when earned. There are three types of split compensation models: the traditional split, the graduated split, and the split to a cap. Let's take a look at all three and which kinds of agents they attract.

The Traditional Split Agent Compensation Model

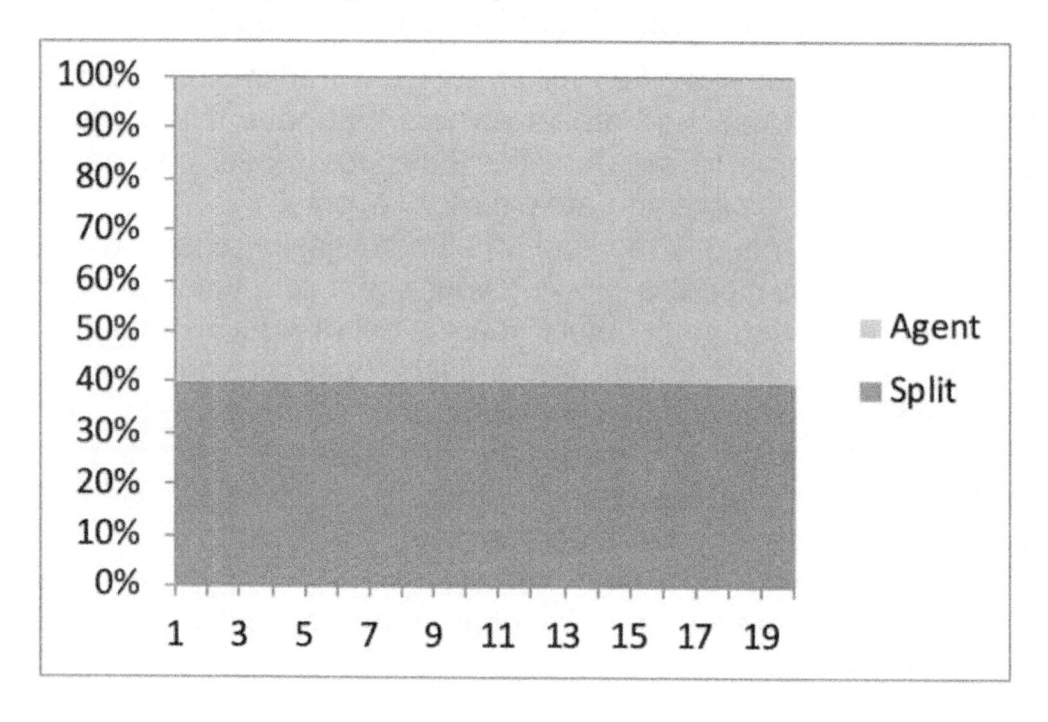

60/40 Split
No CAP

16 Strategies

Traditional split models (split with no cap) are common with small boutique brokerages or brokerages that provide leads to their agents. Traditional splits were more common from 1950-1980, prior to the Monthly Fee and 100% models, like RE/MAX, that became popular in the late 80s and 90s.

Is the Traditional Split Model Right for Your Brokerage?
This compensation model is ideal for you if you are providing leads and/or full service to your agents. This model is also ideal if you want a smaller brokerage of fewer than 10 agents. This is because it is easier to remain profitable when your splits are higher. Another benefit is that you won't have to deal with difficult agent billing.

The challenge with a traditional split will be retaining agents when they become successful and the larger split becomes a burden on their finances. If you want a compensation model that will help retain higher-producing agents, consider the next split option.

The Graduated Split Agent Compensation Model

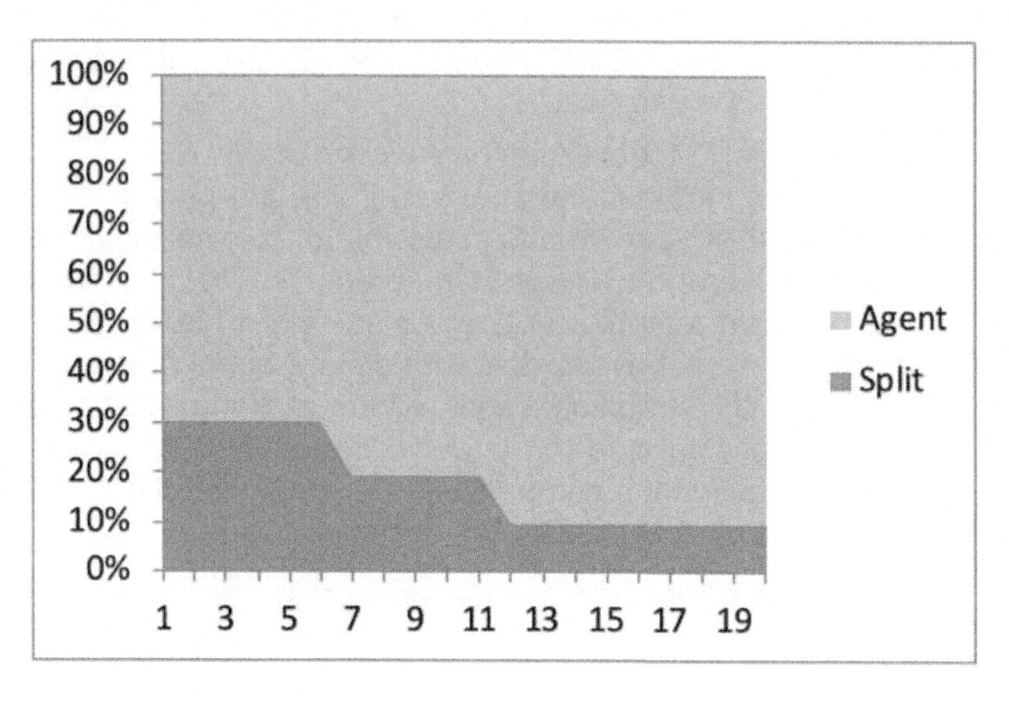

70/30 Split to $60,000 GCI
80/20 Split to $100,000 GCI
90/10 Thereafter

16 Strategies

The graduated split compensation model is similar to the traditional split but allows agents to earn more of the commission when they reach certain milestones. In this example, the agent begins their fiscal year at a 70/30 split, but when the agent reaches $60,000 in gross commissions earned (GCI) they shift to an 80/20 split. Then when they reach the next milestone of $100,000 GCI they earn the 90/10 split for the remainder of their fiscal cycle.

Upon their anniversary the agents' split will reset back to 70/30 or if they can show that they are likely to produce the same or more GCI the next year you may choose to restart them at the higher level of 80/20. This gives the agent motivation to produce and increases retention with your top producers.

Is the Graduated Split Model Right for Your Brokerage?

The graduated split model can be a solution for the retention of top producers that the previous business model is challenged with. This model will also increase your ability to recruit and retain more agents and allow your brokerage to grow well beyond 10 agents.

The Split to a Cap Agent Compensation Model

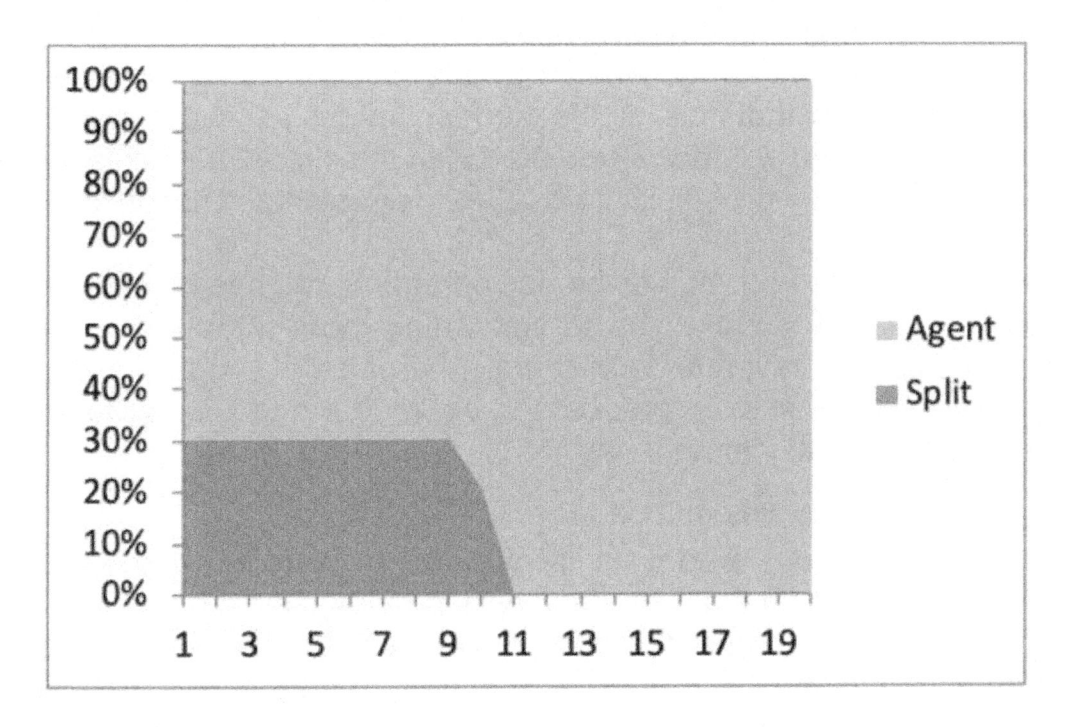

70/30 Split to $30,000 CAP
10.75 Units to CAP

Some brokerages also offer a split to a "cap." The term cap refers to a maximum the agent will pay within the agent's fiscal year. An example of this would be a 70/30 split to a cap of $30,000. This plan allows the agent to pay 30% of commissions earned until the 30% of their commission paid reaches the $30,000 cap.

Once the cap is reached the agent will receive 100% of their commissions for the remainder of their fiscal year, but agents don't traditionally have to guarantee or owe the brokerage the difference if they don't reach the $30,000 cap.

The split to a cap model has become popular because it can support multiple agent types. Keller Williams, Coldwell Banker, and eXp all offer the "split to a cap" model because it allows new agents to start with lower monthly expenses, but it also limits the costs that they will pay the brokerage when they later become a top producer.

You may think that this is the perfect model to follow, but the challenge that you will face if you start with this model is maintaining month-over-month profitability while your agent count is below 40 agents.

This is because your higher-producing agents will cap in just a few months. This will expose you to supporting them without receiving any commission revenue from them. Therefore, I suggest starting with a traditional split or graduated split model and getting to 40+ agents before considering a cap.

Monthly Fee Compensation Models

The **monthly fee model** is similar to a landlord and tenant relationship. The brokerage (landlord) provides all the necessary services the agent needs to be successful with their real estate career in exchange for a fixed monthly fee. The agent (tenant) pays for additional features and services like training, marketing, private office, and transaction coordination separately.

Like a tenant, each agent signs an agreement that they will pay a monthly fee for the brokerage services, and in exchange, they will receive 100% of the commission check when it is earned. This model allows agents to control their costs and have more predictable monthly expenses.

Overall, the monthly fee models charge less than a comparable company's split to a cap model. For example, if a comparable brokerage has a cap of $20,000, your brokerage monthly fee may be $1,200 a month ($1,200 X 12 = $14,400) for similar services. This is because your revenue is essentially guaranteed, and not dependent upon your agents selling a home.

Is the Monthly Fee Model Right for Your Brokerage?

The benefit of the monthly fee model is once you grow your brokerage to the optimal size (10-30 agents), you will have more predictable revenue than the split models. This is because your income is not reliant on the market fluctuations, seasons, or the sales of your agents.

The challenge you will face with the monthly fee model is attracting new, newer, and low-producing agents into your brokerage. **RE/MAX was faced with this in the early 2000s when they discovered that the average age of a RE/MAX agent was much older than the industry's average**.

They feared that if they didn't begin attracting newer agents that they would simply "age-out" as their agents retire. RE/MAX solved this by offering the options of both splits to accommodate newer agents or a fixed monthly fee for the mid-level and top producers.

How to Increase Revenue with Additional Fees

Due to the competitive nature of real estate brokerage, most brokerages have found it difficult to increase their brokerage fees to keep up with inflation. For example, 25 years ago, back when I was a RE/MAX agent, my brokerage charged a monthly fee of $1,100 a month. Here in Colorado in the 1990s, Keller Williams set their cap at $18,000. Due to technology and new competition neither company has raised their brokerage fees in the past 20+ years!

To beat inflation, brokerages have had to increase their agent count, add fees, and offer additional services to find creative ways to generate more revenue. Many of the new services and fees are commonplace for many agents and are a simple way for you to mirror them to create additional revenue for your brokerage.

Additional Fees and Services to Increase Revenue

Fee	Description	Estimated Cost
Agent Transaction Fee	Transaction fee charged to the agent at closing	$100-$250
Buyer Transaction Fee	Transaction fee charged to the buyer at closing	$200-$350
Listing Transaction Fee	Transaction fee charged to the seller at closing	$200-$350
Personal Transaction Fee	Fee for agents on personal transactions, when the agent doesn't take a commission or pay a split	$300-$500
Franchise Fee	Fee paid by agent to the franchisor	5-8% of GCI
Desk Fee	Fee for a reserved desk or area in the office	$50-$150
Office Fee	Fee for a private or shared office (includes desk)	$200-$1000
Brokerage Advertising Fee	Monthly fee paid to support marketing the brokerage	$25/month
Annual Fees	Annual renewal fee	$300-$1,100
Set-up Fees	Fee charged to the agent when they join (includes the first set of business cards, website set-up, and announcement)	$150-$300
Errors and Omissions Ins. Fees	Fee paid monthly, quarterly, annually, or on each transaction to cover the cost of the E&O (This is usually at a profit)	$25-$60/month or $150/transaction
Services		
Transaction Coordination	Contract to closing file management (Optional)	$300-$600/transaction
Showing	Fee charged monthly or per listing	$20/month or

Service Fee		$75/listing
Signs and Lock Boxes	Sign rental and installation (Optional)	$75-$150/listing
Open House Signs	Rented and/or installed (Optional)	$50-$100/listing
Marketing		
Listing Marketing Fee	Listing marketing packages (Optional)	$300-$600/listing
Individual Property Website	Individual property website (Optional)	$50-$100/listing
Listing Presentations	Professional quality printed listing presentation (Optional)	$25-$50/listing
Just Listed/Just Sold Cards	100 cards printed and mailed, includes postage (Optional)	$100-$200/listing
Listing Photography	Professional listing photography, drone photography (Optional)	$150-$400/listing
Training		
New Agent Training	Typically paid with an increased split (Includes materials)	10-20% additional split
Advanced Training	Annual onsite or offsite training events	$50-$500
Mentoring	Typically paid with an increased split	10% additional split
Coaching	Coaching fee is split between coach and brokerage	$500-$1000/month
Continuing Education	Fee includes the cost of instructor, location, and snack	$20/CE credit hour

Common Mistakes to Avoid When Selecting a Compensation Model
There are three common mistakes that are made when selecting your compensation plan and building your brokerage's financial model. They are as follows:

1. Copying Your Current Brokerage

Most real estate agents who decide to start a new brokerage firm will do what I did: take the business model from their former brokerage and try to improve upon it. The mistake you will make by doing this is overlooking the other compensation models that may be a better fit for you as a broker-owner and the types of agents you are wanting to attract to your new brokerage.

2. Offering a Compensation Model to Please All Agents

The difficulty with recruiting real estate agents is that they have different needs at different phases throughout their careers. Newer agents are concerned with training and demand a lot of one-on-one attention. Mid-level agents look for a community and reasonable fees, and top producers and teams need to be able to grow without their expenses growing at a rate faster than revenue.

You may try to come up with a compensation model that serves all agent types no matter what phase of business they are in. This is a grave mistake. When you are incubating your baby brokerage, unless you have millions of dollars to invest, you likely will not have the resources to support all types of agents from the get-go.

I suggest building your brokerage around one agent type first, then you can add in more services and compensation plans to attract a larger variety of agents once you have reached profitability.

3. Overestimating Agent Production

When building your business plan's financial model don't make the overestimation that all of your agents will produce big numbers. This is a common mistake in brokerage business planning.

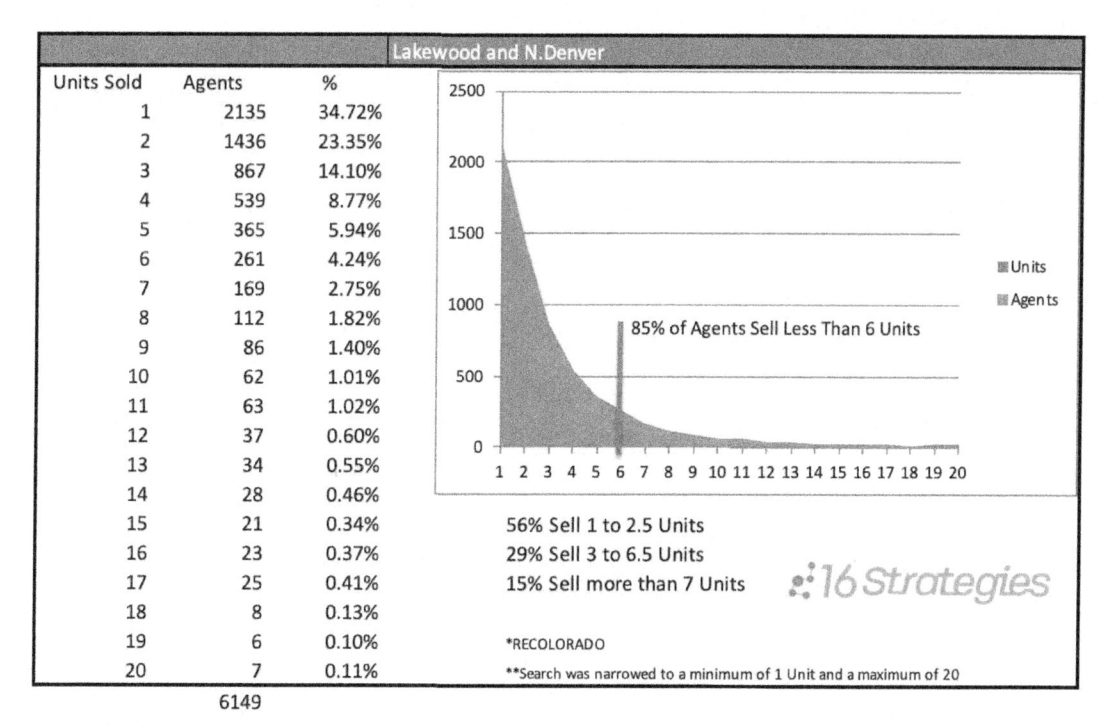

Units Sold	Agents	%
1	2135	34.72%
2	1436	23.35%
3	867	14.10%
4	539	8.77%
5	365	5.94%
6	261	4.24%
7	169	2.75%
8	112	1.82%
9	86	1.40%
10	62	1.01%
11	63	1.02%
12	37	0.60%
13	34	0.55%
14	28	0.46%
15	21	0.34%
16	23	0.37%
17	25	0.41%
18	8	0.13%
19	6	0.10%
20	7	0.11%
	6149	

Lakewood and N. Denver

85% of Agents Sell Less Than 6 Units

56% Sell 1 to 2.5 Units
29% Sell 3 to 6.5 Units
15% Sell more than 7 Units

*RECOLORADO
**Search was narrowed to a minimum of 1 Unit and a maximum of 20

:16 Strategies

In the chart above we looked at the data of 6000 real estate agents in the geographic area around our brokerage in Colorado. We discovered that nearly 35% did less than 1 transaction and the more shocking number is that 85% of all the agents in the area did less than six transactions each year.

You should do this research for your brokerage too. Once you have this data for your area you can create your financial models with more accurate assumptions. If you need help with this BrokerMetrics provides market and agent analysis software that can do this in a snap!

Your Compensation Model Helps Determine Your Business Plan

Brokerage Business Plan

- Commission Model
- Agent Type
- Agent Count
- Agent Services
- Financial Model

16 Strategies

Ultimately, the type of agents you recruit and the amount you choose to charge them will determine the agent count your brokerage will need to reach in order to remain profitable. The type of agent you want to recruit will also determine the services your brokerage will need to provide to attract and retain those agents.

After doing a competitive market analysis of the other brokerages and our previous experience with Keller Williams, we selected the split to a cap Model for our Boulder brokerage. Our compensation model was a $75 Monthly Fee, 70/30 Split to a $18,000 cap, and no Franchise Fee.

The mistake we made is that the split and cap weren't low enough to be attractive to the budget-minded agents who chose to go to the Transaction Fee companies, and it wasn't high enough for us to afford all the additional services of a full-service boutique or luxury brokerage.

This compensation model left us somewhere in the middle of the pack and competing with the large brokerages like RE/MAX,

Coldwell Banker, Keller Williams, and Berkshire Hathaway. If I was to open another boutique-style brokerage today, I would offer a Traditional Split and provide all-inclusive services at no additional cost to the agent. I may even pay for all of the additional fees that agents usually pay such as marketing costs, MLS, E&O Insurance, and REALTOR dues in exchange for a larger share of the commission.

No doubt, this model is more difficult to recruit to, but the additional income from the Traditional Split allows you to continue to provide more customized services than the large brokerages can provide.

The Bottom Line

Once you have determined the compensation model, type of agent you want to recruit, agent count, and services you can determine the overall costs to run that brokerage model. If you find—and you will—that the expenses are higher than you anticipated, you will go back through your plan and adjust your agent count, splits, and fees until you have a profitable business plan supporting the type of agents you want to work with. That is why determining your compensation model is an important step to building a successful real estate brokerage.

12

HOW TO ACCURATELY ESTIMATE EXPENSES

Opening your own brokerage is a huge milestone in your real estate career. However, if you don't accurately estimate your expenses your brokerage dream will quickly become a nightmare.

Many agents say that the expense of running a brokerage is similar to running a team. This is far from reality. In a real estate brokerage, you will have additional expenses that cost much more to provide than you would expect.

When your brokerage is just starting out you will need to keep a close eye on your expenses. You won't be able to avoid some of the upfront expenses, but some of the other costs can be added later as your brokerage grows.

This chapter is to help you prepare for all the expenses, the following chapter will help you come up with a realistic budget to run a profitable real estate brokerage.

Real Estate Brokerage Expense Categories

I will review all the possible expenses you may incur operating a real estate brokerage. Each of the categories below represents a group of expenses along with their estimated annual cost and their ideal percentage of your overall revenue.

Each category will be broken down and explained in detail later in this chapter. After you have reviewed each of your brokerage's expenses you can move to estimating your revenues and completing your real estate brokerages budget worksheet later.

REAL ESTATE BROKERAGE EXPENSES

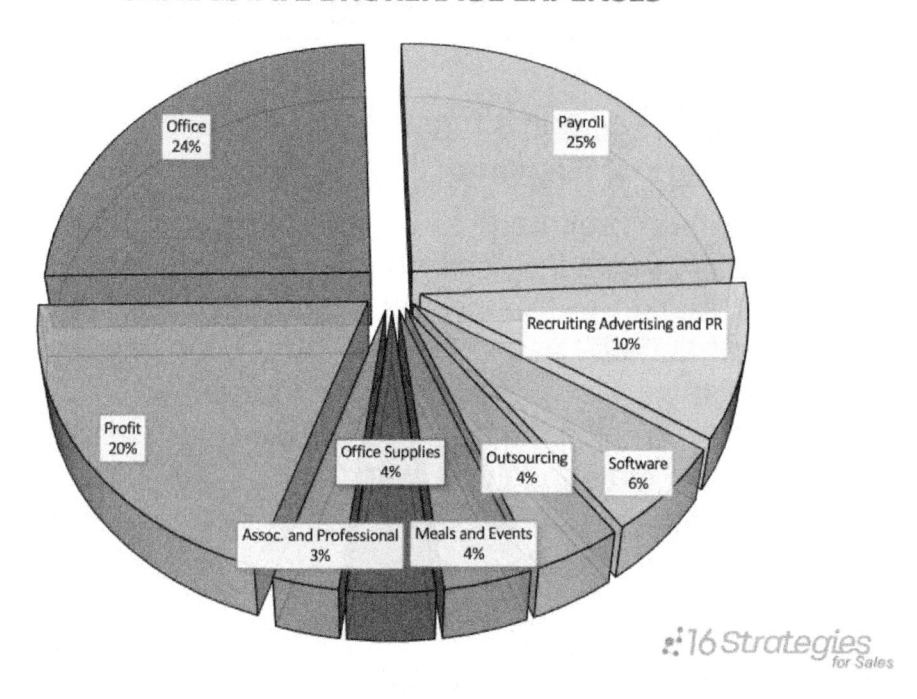

Pie chart segments:
- Payroll 25%
- Office 24%
- Profit 20%
- Recruiting Advertising and PR 10%
- Software 6%
- Office Supplies 4%
- Outsourcing 4%
- Meals and Events 4%
- Assoc. and Professional 3%

Real Estate Brokerage Expense Categories

Expense Category	Estimated Annual Costs	Ideal Percentage of Revenue
Payroll	$45,000-$120,000	25%-30%
Outsourcing	$18,000-$24,000	18%-25%
Software	$13,000-$36,000	3%-6%
Office	($0 Virtual) $80,000-$260,000/Yr	(0% Virtual) 20%-30%
Advertising (Buyer and Seller Leads)	$20,000-$100,000	(Excluded from operational budget)
Associations, Insurance, and Professional Fees.	$12,000-$18,000/Yr	2%-4%
Recruiting, Advertising, and PR	$6,000-$60,000	5%-10%
Meals and Events	$9,000-$24,000	2%-5%

| Office Supplies | $12,000-$24,000/Yr | 3%-8% |
| Profit | $120,000-$360,000 | 15%-20% |

Payroll Expenses

Estimated Cost: $45,000-$120,000/Yr
Ideal Percentage of Revenue: 20%-30%

Your real estate brokerage's payroll expense may vary across several different variables. The number of employees you have, the employment market in the city your brokerage will be located, and the additional benefits you choose to offer your employees are just three examples.

Adding insult to injury, many new brokers forget to factor in the other expenses that go along with payroll like family leave time, insurance, and payroll taxes.

Employee Payroll

Estimate: $32,000-$96,000/Yr

The number of employees you have at any given time is dependent on the services you are offering to attract agents and the size of your brokerage. For deeper insight on which employees to hire at different stages of growth.

The city and state you are opening your brokerage in will also affect the cost of payroll for your brokerage. Even the cost of a receptionist can vary greatly between a city like Chicago and a rural town like Wichita. To get an accurate estimate of the costs to hire in your area you will need to do some research on average salaries in the area.

Additional Benefits

Estimate: $3,200-$9,600/Yr

Remember to factor in additional employee benefits like health insurance, life insurance, PTO (vacation), family leave, 401(k) contributions, and bonuses. If overlooked in your budget, these expenses can surprise you later and throw off your profitability.

Decide now what your policy is for vacation days, PTO, family leave days, and if you are contributing to a 401(k).

Employer Payroll Tax
Estimate: $2,700-$8,100/Yr

The most common expense new broker-owners overlook is the additional taxes that are required to be paid by the employer. Let me tell you, the IRS doesn't take kindly to businesses that fail to pay employment taxes. In addition to the hourly wage or salary that you agree to pay your employees, you, the employer, must also pay Employer Payroll Tax. This is an additional 7.65% that your brokerage pays to Medicare and Social Security.

Workers Compensation Insurance
Estimate: $560-$1680/Yr

Most states also require employers to provide Workers Compensation Insurance. Failing to do so may result in significant fines or even closure. Worker's Compensation Insurance protects the employee and you in the event that your employee gets injured on the job and isn't able to work.

Payroll Servicing Company
Estimate: $900-$2,700/Yr

If all this is giving you a headache, you can hand off all your payroll worries to a Payroll Servicing Company. These companies will handle all the state and national requirements for hiring and managing employees, including legal requirements, tax withholding, and Worker's Compensation Insurance. Just be sure to count the additional expense for the Payroll Servicing into your budget.

Outsourcing Transaction Coordination, File Review, & Other Expenses
Estimated Cost: $18,000-$24,000/Yr
Ideal Percentage of Revenue: 3%-5%

In an effort to keep your employee costs low, consider outsourcing as much as you can from the beginning. Fortunately, brokerage tasks like transaction management and brokerage file review can easily be outsourced.

Transaction coordinator companies charge between $150-$300 a file depending on the volume you will be sending them. If money is tight, you might consider paying a detail-minded, experienced agent that's in your brokerage to do it on the side for less.

While you're at it, consider outsourcing other agent services like photography, marketing, or sign installation and storage.

Software Expenses
Estimated Cost: $13,000-$36,000/Yr
Ideal Percentage of Revenue: 3%-6%

Gone are the days of having four to five employees to run your real estate brokerage. Today many of the services brokerages provide are managed with software. This allows you to run your brokerage with as few as just one employee.

Since there are so many options for brokerage software available today, estimating these expenses can be tricky.

For now, here is a quick breakdown of rough estimates for software pricing in common categories you will likely need:

Software	Description	Estimated Annual Cost
Showing Service	Set and coordinate showings, manage feedback.	$240-$540/Agent or $20/Listing
MLS	Managing Broker Multiple Listing Service access.	$240-$480/Yr
CRM or All-In-One Solution	Contact Management Software or All-in-One CRM/Website Solution	$180/Agent/Yr
Websites	Brokerage website and individual agent websites.	$144-$2,400/Yr
Digital	Software to assist agents or the Marketing	$168/Agent or

Marketing Suite	Coordinator to create and manage agents and listing marketing.	$2,400/Yr
Transaction Management	Collects and manages required documentation and signatures on behalf of the brokerage.	$85/Agent or $2,400/Yr +
Financial Management	Manages and tracks agent fees and caps, manages brokerage expenses and revenue, and prepares documentation for tax preparation.	$2,400-$3,600/Yr
Paperless Contract Software	Paperless real estate contact software.	$120/Agent
Agent Recruiting Software	Measures and tracks agent performance through the MLS and CRM with proven recruiting templates.	$2,400-$3,600/Yr
Total Annual Cost		$13,000-$36,000

Office & Office Related Expenses

Estimated Cost: ($0 Virtual) $80,000-$260,000/Yr

Ideal Percentage of Revenue: (0% Virtual) 20%-30%

Unless your real estate brokerage is going to operate virtually (without an office), your office will likely take up a large chunk of your expenses.

Since there are so many factors to consider, choosing the right office can be challenging, Some factors are obvious, but many are not so obvious and only reveal themselves after you've signed the lease.

For expense purposes, the costs associated with a brick-and-mortar real estate office can be broken down into four categories: base rent, CAM, utilities, and maintenance.

Base Rent

Estimated Cost: $36,000-$66,000/Yr

The Base Rent is the amount your brokerage must pay each month for the use of the space. Typical office space today in a city like Boulder, Colorado can range anywhere from $25 to $50+ per square foot. To do a Base Rent square foot calculation on commercial lease space you need to take the total square footage of the portion of the building you are leasing and multiply it by the cost per square foot.

So if you're looking at an office space that is 3000 square feet and they are asking $22 a foot for base rent then your cost would be $66,000 a year in annual base rent. (3000sq ft X $22sq ft = $66,000). Divide the annual base rent by 12 and you will have your monthly base rent ($66,000/12 = $5,500 monthly base rent).

Common Area Maintenance

Estimated Cost: $15,000-$30,000/Yr

Common Area Maintenance (CAM) fees are additional expenses that are associated with the property that are passed through to the tenant. These additional expenses include costs that directly relate to the space you occupy PLUS the expenses related to the rest of the property like parking lots or common areas.

Common CAM expenses are cleaning, repairs, building maintenance, utilities, internet, insurance, security, parking lot maintenance, snow removal, landscaping, trash, and taxes.

CAM fees can add an additional $7-$12 a square foot to your lease, and you can even be back charged if the CAM was underestimated. So, before you sign that lease make sure you understand your liability and what you can afford.

Utilities

Estimated Cost: $3000-$13,000/Yr

If your lease or CAM doesn't include utilities you will need to budget for them as well. When you budget for utilities you may only think of gas, electricity, water, and sewer. However, if you are planning on making calls and going online you will need to budget for communication utilities like phone and internet. These can add up quickly.

Maintenance
Estimated Cost: $1,500-$3,000/Yr

If everything goes as planned with your brokerage and why shouldn't it… you will have lots of wear and tear from busy agents using your office. To keep things in ship shape you will want to budget for common maintenance. This can include services like cleaning, trash removal, recycling, and paper shredding.

If you are renting a stand-alone building or building maintenance isn't covered in your lease or CAM, then you will want to budget for additional building maintenance to ensure your agents and their clients aren't turned off by a poorly maintained office.

Cleaning
Estimated Costs: $4,800/Yr

Of course, you or your staff can take the time once a week to clean your office, but in time it will be seen by your employees more as a punishment than a required task. The cost of hiring a cleaning service will give you an instant ROI from a happier staff.

I would be remiss not to mention that Covid-19 has added more awareness to the cleanliness of our workplaces. This additional attention to cleanliness is leading to more specific cleaning techniques and an overall higher cost.

Buyer and Seller Lead Advertising Costs
Estimated Cost: $20,000-$100,000/Yr
Estimated Return: $40,000-$400,000
Percentage of Revenue: (Excluded from Operational Budget)

While providing buyer and seller leads certainly isn't required to operate a brokerage, many brokerages today provide some brokerage referred leads or lead programs.

To help manage this, many tech-savvy brokerages are using all-in-one CRM/website and lead management software platforms like Real Geeks to generate leads. The cost of systems like these ranges from $500 to over $2,500 a month not including the cost of advertising. The advertising spend necessary to generate a consistent return starts at $1,000 a month and can quickly exceed $10,000 a month.

If you're looking for a more hands-off approach, you can buy leads directly for your agents from services like Zillow or BoldLeads.

In order to maximize your ROI from leads you buy for your agents, you might want to consider hiring a Leads Manager to manage the system, track leads, and keep agents accountable. This one hire can increase your ROI from paid leads to 300-400% of your costs.

Separate Profit and Loss Statement

Instead of including the cost of the system, advertising, and Leads Manager in your brokerage's operational budget, I recommend having a separate profit and loss statement for the leads program. This P&L will combine the expenses of running the program with the revenue received as referral fees that agents pay when they close a transaction referred from the leads program. This P&L will quickly show if the program is operating profitably.

Associations, Professional, & Insurance Expenses

Estimated Cost: $12,000-$18,000/Yr
Ideal Percentage of Revenue: 2%-4%

Some expenses to run your real estate brokerage are necessary but are far less exciting than renting a flashy office. Unavoidable expenses like insurance, banking, and legal come to mind.

Additionally, expenses like membership dues, licensing fees, and tax preparation can easily be overlooked because they only occur once a year. To create a comprehensive budget you will need to remember to include each of these as the costs can be significant.

Here is a quick breakdown of the expenses associated with licensing, insurance, and other professional costs:

Category	Item	Estimated Cost
Licensing		
	Brokerage License Fees (State)	$550/Yr
	Business License (City)	$300/Yr
	Use Taxes and Fees (City)	$150/Yr
Insurance		
	Errors and Omissions Insurance (Group Policy < 25 Agents)	$3500/Yr
	Liability Insurance	$400/Yr
	Property and Casualty Insurance	$600/Yr
Memberships		
	Association of REALTORS	$600/Yr
	Chamber of Commerce	$900/Yr
Legal		
	Real Estate Attorney	$1200/Yr
	Corporate Attorney	$300/Yr
Accounting		
	Bookkeeper	$600/Yr
	Tax Preparation	$1200/Yr
Bank Charges		
	Account Fees	$300/Yr
Total Annual Cost		**$10,600**

Recruiting, Advertising, & PR Costs
Estimated Cost: $6,000-$60,000/Yr
Ideal Percentage of Revenue: 5%-10%

Recruiting, advertising, and PR expenses will also take a significant chunk of your revenue each month. Here are some quick estimates of common expenses associated with recruiting, advertising, and PR:

Agent Recruiting Ads

Estimated Cost: $3,000-$6,000/Yr

Even if you do no other advertising, if you wish to grow your brokerage rapidly you will want to budget for agent wanted ads on websites like Indeed, Zip Recruiter, and Craigslist. These websites charge between $25 (Craigslist) to $400+ a month to run help wanted ads.

Newspaper Display Ads and Press Releases

Estimated Cost: $0-$24,000/Yr

Yes... The newspaper IS still an effective way to promote your brokerage and your listings. This is especially true in high-traffic tourist destinations, small towns, and areas where the average population is older. To save money, negotiate your display ads for 6-12-month agreements instead of weekly.

When your agents feel appreciated, they will stay. The best way to welcome a new agent aboard or to celebrate an agent's accomplishments is to do paid press releases. Most newspapers will do these for a few hundred dollars. Take my word for it... it's totally worth it!

Signs, Swag, and Business Cards

Estimated Cost: $1,000-$8,000/Yr

Printing, storing, and managing your brokerage's listing signs and open house signs will not only make your agents happier, it will also help you maintain your brand image and standards. Contract with a sign company for a volume discount.

Physical swag like custom pens, coffee mugs, shirts, hats, or umbrellas can also go a long way to helping you promote your brand

and make your agents feel part of a team.

Another outstanding way to maintain your brand while standing out from the brokerages that make agents pay for *evvvvverything,* is to provide business cards for your agents. It is a low-cost and simple gesture that agents will cherish.

Social Media and Google Remarketing
Estimated Cost: $3,000-$22,000/Yr

Build your brand awareness by having a solid remarketing campaign on both Google and Facebook. A remarketing campaign will advertise your brokerage to visitors that landed on your website. This will not only build your brokerage brand with the community but with new potential agents.

Also don't miss the opportunity to set up your Google Business and Yelp for Business accounts. Both of these will help consumers find your brokerage quickly.

Meals and Event Expenses
Estimated Cost: $9,000-$24,000/Yr
Ideal Percentage of Revenue: 2%-5%

Unless you want to be personally footing the bill each time you meet a potential recruit or have a team meeting (guilty!) you will need to include meals and events in your expenses.

Here is a quick breakdown of estimated expenses for meals and events for a small brokerage:

Event	Frequency	Estimated Cost
Recruiting and Retention: Coffee and lunches with recruits or your agents.	Twice a Week	$20-$50/each
Team Meetings	Weekly	$75-$150/each. (Consider getting sponsors.)
Training Events: CE Classes, Software Training, Contract	Monthly	$150-$250/each. (Consider getting sponsors.)

Classes, etc.		
Large Events: Speaking Events, Award Ceremonies, Recruiting Events, Client Appreciation Parties	Quarterly	$1000-$4000/each Includes: Event space, speaker, coffee, and snacks. (Consider getting sponsors.)
Holiday Party	Annually	$2500-$7000. Includes: Event space, catering, entertainment, and drinks.
Total Annual Cost		$9,000-$24,000 (Including 50% Sponsorship)

Find Sponsors for Your Events

Consider finding sponsors to assist with the cost for your events that are not intimate or contain confidential information. Most states allow for mortgage and title companies to pay a small portion depending on the number of agents that are in the room, or they may allow them to pay for a booth or an opportunity to speak to your group. Other vendors like property inspectors, solar companies, and movers are less regulated and are happy to help with the cost for an opportunity to meet your busy agents.

Just don't expect to make money on your events or even to get 100% of the costs covered by sponsors. A good practice is to estimate that you will have up to 50% of the costs covered by sponsors.

Office Supplies & Other Office Expenses
Estimated Annual Cost: $12,000-$24,000/Yr
Ideal Percentage of Revenue: 3%-8%

The expenses related to office supplies have decreased dramatically this year, but they can still be significant. Yet, if you are building a full-service brokerage you still want to be prepared to support the busy agent that needs their marketing and presentations professionally printed and bound.

You will also have some costs related to your part-time and full-time employees that are working at the office each day.

Coffee and Filtered Water

Estimated Costs: $1,500/Yr

Truth be told, I love coffee and I am a coffee snob. Brokerages that don't provide their employees and agents quality coffee and filtered water is like saying, *"We actually don't want you here!"* Do yourself and your team a favor and spend a little on the little things that matter. Coffee and water service companies like Lavazza will keep you stocked up and prevent you from having to run to the store for coffee 5-minutes before the team meeting.

Office Supplies and Paper

Estimated Costs: $1200/Yr

The cost of pens, paper, and Post-It notes add up and if not managed can quickly eat up your profits. To keep office spending under control, set a monthly budget so everyone knows where the spending limit is.

Copy Machine and Ink

Estimated Costs: $3600/Yr

You may find this shocking, but a top-of-the-line copy machine today can cost as much as a well-equipped Honda Civic! Copy machine companies will do their best to tie you into a long-term lease on a new machine for $600-$900 a month!

They will tell you that you will save money over time. What they don't tell you is that the cost of the lease usually doesn't cover the full cost of the Ink. They will say things like, "Ink is only 3¢ a page" what they don't say is that a color page uses 4 ink colors per page. This means that each color page costs 12¢ a page, and this is in addition to the cost of leasing the copier.

To keep your budget within reason, I suggest finding a used copier for $3000-$5000 and paying for a maintenance contract for

$200-$300 a month that includes ink for a limited number of copies.

Shredding

Estimated Costs: $480/Yr

With identity theft on an all-time high, shredding confidential printed documentation is a must.

Profit as an Expense

Most people don't think of profit as an expense. But if you wish to build an accurate budget for your real estate brokerage you will need to factor in profit into your expenses. Think of it this way, if you sold a bushel of apples for $10 at the local farmers market, that $10 is your revenue, not your profit. Because you have expenses related to acquiring and selling the apples, right?

Say the cost of buying the apples from a local organic farmer costs you $5 and then you spend $2 on cleaning them and placing them in a nice bushel. Your cost of goods is $7. However, you also have other expenses like gas and the rent on your space at the farmer's market to consider. These two expenses run you an additional $60 a month.

So, What's Your Profit?

Well, your profit will depend on how many bushels of apples you sell, right? So to determine how many apples you must sell each month you must first determine how much profit you wish to make.

Let's say you wish to make $300 a month in profit selling apples at the market. Knowing that the cost of goods is $7 a bushel and our monthly expenses are $60 a month we can now calculate that you must sell 120 bushels each month to make $300 in profit.

Creating your budget for your real estate brokerage is no different. Decide on an amount or percentage of profit that you wish to achieve each year and add it into your expenses before estimating your revenue.

The Bottom Line

There are dozens of possible expenses you may incur operating a real estate brokerage. However, thinking through your expenses upfront is essential. Once you complete that, you can move to the fun part: estimating your real estate brokerage revenues and finalizing your real estate brokerage budget.

13

BROKERAGE BUDGET AND MAXIMIZING PROFITABILITY

By this point, about 75% of the wannabe broker-owners have either given up or have decided that all this planning is too much work and they are going to figure it out as they go. To that, I say (sarcastically) good luck!

For those of you who have stuck it out this far, I am sure you are going to be one of the few that become a huge success! This is the most important chapter and everything we have been working on thus far will now come together, as you will put together your brokerage's budget.

There are many things you must consider when creating the budget for your brokerage. Expenses, revenue estimates, splits and fees, and agent count to name a few. Common mistakes new brokerage owners make is overlooking expenses or overestimating revenue. Doing either of these may lead to you losing money, or even worse utter failure. To give you the best chance for success I created my real estate brokerage budget worksheet to help you get started with your budget without missing a step.

Step 1: Download the Brokerage Budget Worksheet

REVENUE	Jan	Feb	Mar	Apr	May	Jun	Jul	Aug	Sept	Oct	Nov	Dec	
Total Agent Count	10	11	12	13	14	15	16	17	18	19	20	21	
Split Income	$34,320	$37,752	$41,184	$44,616	$48,048	$51,480	$54,912	$58,344	$61,776	$65,208	$68,640	$72,072	$638,352
Monthly Bill	$500	$550	$600	$650	$700	$750	$800	$850	$900	$950	$1,000	$1,050	$9,300
Agent Office Rent	$200	$200	$250	$250	$300	$300	$350	$350	$400	$400	$450	$450	$3,900
Additional Services Income	$0	$0	$0	$0	$0	$0	$0	$0	$0	$0	$0	$0	$0
Vendor Rental Income	$0	$0	$0	$0	$0	$0	$0	$0	$0	$0	$0	$0	$0
Total Income	$35,020	$38,502	$42,034	$45,516	$49,048	$52,530	$56,062	$59,544	$63,076	$66,558	$70,090	$73,572	$651,552
1. Payroll													
Operations Manager	$3,800	$3,800	$3,800	$3,800	$3,800	$3,800	$3,800	$3,800	$3,800	$3,800	$3,800	$3,800	$45,600
Marketing Manager	$0	$0	$0	$0	$0	$0	$0	$0	$0	$0	$0	$0	$0
Sales Manager	$4,000	$4,000	$4,000	$4,000	$4,000	$4,000	$4,000	$4,000	$4,000	$4,000	$4,000	$4,000	$48,000
Sales Manager Bonus	$0	$200	$200	$200	$200	$200	$200	$200	$200	$200	$200	$200	$2,200
Transaction Coordinator	$0	$0	$0	$0	$0	$0	$0	$0	$0	$0	$0	$0	$0
File Auditor	$300	$300	$350	$350	$400	$400	$450	$450	$500	$500	$550	$550	$5,100
Payroll Services	$75	$75	$75	$75	$75	$75	$75	$75	$75	$75	$75	$75	$900
Payroll Total	$8,175	$8,375	$8,425	$8,425	$8,475	$8,475	$8,525	$8,525	$8,575	$8,575	$8,625	$8,625	$101,800
2. Office and Office Expenses													
Rent	$3,000	$3,000	$3,000	$3,000	$3,000	$3,000	$3,000	$3,000	$3,000	$3,000	$3,000	$3,000	$36,000
CAM and Utility Charges	$350	$350	$350	$350	$350	$350	$350	$350	$350	$350	$350	$350	$4,200
Maintainance	$50	$50	$50	$50	$50	$50	$50	$50	$50	$50	$50	$50	$600
Phones	$150	$150	$150	$150	$150	$150	$150	$150	$150	$150	$150	$150	$1,800
Internet	$60	$60	$60	$60	$60	$60	$60	$60	$60	$60	$60	$60	$720
Cleaning	$200	$200	$200	$200	$200	$200	$200	$200	$200	$200	$200	$200	$2,400
Office Total	$3,810	$3,810	$3,810	$3,810	$3,810	$3,810	$3,810	$3,810	$3,810	$3,810	$3,810	$3,810	$45,720
3. Software													
Showing Service	$75	$75	$100	$100	$125	$125	$150	$150	$175	$175	$200	$200	$1,650
MLS	$40	$40	$40	$40	$40	$40	$40	$40	$40	$40	$40	$40	$480
CRM	$150	$180	$210	$240	$270	$300	$330	$360	$390	$420	$450	$480	$3,780
Websites	$75	$75	$75	$75	$75	$75	$75	$75	$75	$75	$75	$75	$900
Digital Marketing Suite	$200	$200	$200	$200	$200	$200	$200	$200	$200	$200	$200	$200	$2,400
Transaction Management	$200	$200	$200	$200	$200	$200	$200	$200	$200	$200	$200	$200	$2,400
Financial Management	$200	$200	$200	$200	$200	$200	$200	$200	$200	$200	$200	$200	$2,400
Contract Software	$0	$0	$0	$0	$0	$0	$0	$0	$0	$0	$0	$0	$0
Recruiting Software	$0	$0	$0	$0	$0	$0	$0	$0	$0	$0	$0	$0	$0
Software Total	$940	$970	$1,025	$1,055	$1,110	$1,140	$1,195	$1,225	$1,280	$1,310	$1,365	$1,395	$14,010
4. Advertising and PR													

Fortunately, you won't need to start from scratch to build your real estate brokerage budget, because I have already done the hard work for you. Start by downloading the **Real Estate Brokerage Budget Worksheet** at https://theclose.com/brokerage-resources

After you have downloaded the worksheet and reviewed the columns, I will walk you through how to fill out each section by adding some assumptions, then expenses, and finally estimated revenues. Feel free to add or subtract expenses to modify the worksheet for your needs.

Step 2: Add Your Brokerage Assumptions

You will need to do some research and make some assumptions about your market and what you believe your average agents' production will be. These estimates will be used later to calculate your brokerage's earnings. Be careful not to overestimate these.

For instance, when you're estimating the Average Sales Price you may use 80% of the average sales price of the area if you are a buyer-heavy brokerage and 90% if you are a listing heavy brokerage.

When it comes to your budget, you are often better off underestimating the income and overestimating the expenses. Ideally, your budget is conservative so you are easily able to surpass the expectations. This ensures that you will have the money and resources to achieve your ultimate goal.

Add Your Brokerage Assumptions into the Worksheet

Step 2

Average Sales Price	$400,000
Average Transactions Per Agent	5
Average Commission %	
Average Commission $	$10,000
Brokerage Split	30%
Monthly Office Bill	$50

Using the Real Estate Brokerage Budget Worksheet, add what you believe the Average Sales Price and the Average Transactions your agents will produce each year. Then input the Average Commission Percentage your agents will charge.

Next, add the splits and fees that you have determined your brokerage will charge. If you are not charging either a split or monthly office bill you can leave it blank. If you are charging your agents a monthly fee for E&O, you can also add it here.

Once you finish adding your assumptions, it's time to move on to your expenses.

Step 3: Calculate the Expenses to Run Your Brokerage

Your brokerage's total annual expenses are the sum of all the expenses to run your real estate brokerage for a full year. This includes payroll, software, staff, office, office supplies, and advertising.

Once you have them together add them to the budget worksheet.

Enter Your Expenses into the Worksheet

Step 3

1. Payroll	
Operations Manager	$3,800
Marketing Manager	$0
Sales Manager	$4,000
Sales Manager Bonus	$0
Transaction Coordinator	$0
File Auditor	$300
Payroll Services	$75
Payroll Total	**$8,175**
2. Office and Office Expenses	
Rent	$3,000
CAM and Utility Charges	$350
Maintainance	$50
Phones	$150
Internet	$60
Cleaning	$200
Office Total	**$3,810**

Working your way through the worksheet you will enter the appropriate monthly expenses into the correct month and category. The worksheet will automatically calculate the year-end totals.

Fixed Expenses vs Variable Expenses

Notice that you may have both fixed and variable expenses. Fixed expenses are expenses that don't fluctuate month to month, like rent and payroll. Variable expenses are expenses that fluctuate based on sales, agent count, or seasonality. These are expenses like photography, training events, agent websites, and association dues.

Take your time here to ensure you are accounting for all your brokerages expenses. CAM charges, coffee and snacks, and cleaning the office are often things that are overlooked. Each section will automatically calculate a monthly expense and total to the right.

Next, you will estimate your theoretical agent count and closings.

Step 4: Project Your Agent Count and Closings

As we discussed earlier, the average agent sells fewer than ten homes a year and it's no secret that newer agents sell fewer and less expensive homes than agents that have been in the business for 5-10 years.

Therefore, if your brokerage is geared towards newer agents, you will need more of them in order to generate enough closings and revenue to cover your expenses.

Estimate Your Agent Count in Your Budget Worksheet

Step 4

REVENUE	Jan	Feb
Total Agent Count	10	11
Closings	4.17	4.58

Using the worksheet, estimate your month-over-month agent count. Be conservative in your estimates. Keep in mind that you will have some agents that won't ever produce and some agents that will leave your brokerage.

When you enter your agents, the worksheet will automatically calculate the closings and commission income based on the estimates you entered in Step 2. If you wish to make an adjustment to the number of closings your agents close you can return to Step 2 and adjust the Average Transactions Per Agent.

Once you have completed your month-over-month agent count, move to the revenue section to complete the budget worksheet.

Step 5: Estimate Your New Brokerages Revenue

The commission income you earn from your personal sales should not support the brokerage. This is a common mistake many brokerage owners make by supporting their brokerage with their own income. The reason you cannot do this is it will prevent you from being able to sell the business in the future.

For most business owners, the reason you started the business was to build an asset that one day could be passed on or sold. Otherwise, why would you go through all the hassles of creating and building a brokerage? The type of agent you choose to recruit and the size of your brokerage will greatly determine your real estate brokerage's overall profitability.

Your brokerage's revenue will come from the splits and fees you will charge your agents. If you are a brokerage owner who also sells real estate then build your budget with you as an agent that pays a full fee just like any other agent.

Additional revenue sources can come from renting office space to your agents or vendors like mortgage, insurance, and in some stated title and escrow companies.

Now you will estimate your revenue to determine your profitability.

Enter your Revenue into the Budget Worksheet

Step 5

Split Income	$12,500
Monthly Bill	$500
Agent Office Rent	$200
Agent Services Income	$0
Additional Income	$0
Total Income	**$13,200**

The Split Income and Monthly Bill will automatically calculate from the estimates you provided in Step 2. If your real estate brokerage has office space and offers shared or private office space for rent, add this into the worksheet under Agent Office Rent.

Agent Services Income is the revenue your brokerage will receive for providing additional services like transaction coordination, marketing services, and training. Estimate and insert this additional revenue into the worksheet.

Don't forget to account for additional revenue opportunities like training and event sponsorships, vendor marketing agreements, and renting out your extra office space.

Step 6: Calculate Your Profit!

Congratulations, you have finished your budget! Now you may have noticed that your profitability isn't what you had hoped, or you may even be showing a loss. It is normal for a startup business to lose money for a few months or even years.

The secret is knowing what your loss is and being prepared by having enough money set aside to cover the losses until you are consistently profitable.

Making Adjustments to your Budget

	Nov	Dec	TOTAL PROFIT
Income Vs Expenses TOTALS	$22,920	$19,915	$161,430

If you're losing more money than you are comfortable with then you may need to make some adjustments to your business plan or budget. Be cautious when you are adjusting your budget. It is easy to get swept up in the possibilities of success and overlook the actual difficulty of achieving some of your goals.

Keep a clear head and have someone else review your budget for optimistic assumptions and inaccuracies. Here are some tips to follow when making adjustments to your budget.

Services and Software

Review your services. Are there services that agents can just as easily provide for themselves, like a low-cost CRM? If so, you may be able to save the expense today and provide it later once your brokerage and budget get a little larger.

I have found that most agents don't or won't use the CRM their brokerage provides. This makes it an easy item to cut from your expenses and add it to a later phase.

Staff

Fewer services and software also means less staff to fulfill the offerings or to train on the software. Start your brokerage lean and mean, and utilize part-time and outsourcing when possible.

Office Space

Sadly the *"Build it and they will come!"* mentality has doomed many potentially profitable new brokerages. They think splashing out on expensive office space will help them attract top-producing agents right out of the gate. Don't fall for this. You are better off starting in a lower quality building or location and attracting agents on your services and culture than you are renting an expensive office only to find out that agents don't value the services you're offering or your splits and fees.

Splits, Fees, and Agent Count

It is easy to correct your budget by overestimating your splits, fees, and agent count. Therefore, don't adjust these until you are confident that your services warrant the fees you are charging, and you can recruit agents to your brokerage's agent compensation plan.

The Bottom Line

As a coach, broker-owner, franchisee, and franchisor, I have created hundreds of budgets for both brokerages and large teams. What I can tell you is if you don't set expectations for your brokerage you will have little or no chance of achieving your goals.

There are many well-intentioned brokerage owners who believe that one day their brokerage will grow beyond their city, state, and possibly the country. After years and years of operating their brokerage, they are no closer to that dream. It isn't that they don't have a good brand or outstanding business model. It's because they are not holding themselves accountable to the plan. **Ideas without execution are just dreams.**

I'm sure you've heard the saying, "You can't manage what you don't measure." If you don't have a clear budget you won't have clear milestones to guide your business. Your budget can act as your business plan, guide your goals, and manage your expenses.

14

CREATE AN AGENT ATTRACTION STORY

Many have tried to open a real estate brokerage and failed. They fail because they simply don't have a clear and powerful story. When they meet with a prospective associate to join their firm, their message falls flat leaving the recruit to wonder why they wasted their time.

How do I know this to be true? Well, because over the past 10 years I have recruited over 400 agents to my brokerages and I have coached many others to successfully recruit to theirs. So I can say without a doubt, that if you own a real estate brokerage or team or are thinking about starting a real estate brokerage then you must have an impactful message.

I'll show you exactly how to craft a powerful message that will attract producing agents to your brokerage.

Get Clear on What's Important to You

The first step to crafting your story is to figure out what's truly important to you. Producing agents have their pick of brokerages to join, which means their choice can often be an emotional one. What is it about your brokerage that will attract them? To get clear, start with these questions: *Why does your brokerage exist and how is it different from the other brokerages?*

The answers to these two questions should be easy if you created your brokerage but may be more challenging if you work for an existing brokerage.

Maybe your brokerage was created because the industry was getting away from high-level service to the agents or the customers and you saw an opportunity to provide better service. Or was it that you wanted to specialize in a specific neighborhood that is up and coming or underserved? Whatever the reason you must be super clear on what it is and why it is important to you.

If you didn't build your brokerage then do this exercise by reviewing your company's Mission, Vision, and Values and ask yourself what about this excites you and why are these things important to you.

Examples: Reasons Your Brokerage Exists

- To achieve #1 in market share in Des Moines IA
- To provide a luxury experience
- To create WOW in our clients' worlds
- To save our clients' money
- To promote and preserve the *Mission Beach* lifestyle

When you get clear on why your brokerage exists and more importantly why this is important to you, your passion will show through when you talk about your brokerage. You won't need to "sell" your brokerage because your passion and excitement will do the selling for you in the recruiting appointment.

Craft a Story That Excites

We are all on this planet for a limited period of time and nobody wants to waste it in a meaningless way. When we reflect on our lives, we want to say that we accomplished something and that we made an impact in some way. This is your life story. Don't you want it to be a compelling story?

Your brokerage also needs a story. One that inspires and excites the kind of people you want to work with. You don't need or want every real estate agent to join your brokerage. In fact, you only want the agents that share the common interest, value, or view that your brokerage exists to promote.

To successfully attract producing agents, you need to craft a story that excites them to want to come along on your journey. There are five parts to crafting a powerful story. Your brokerage's story begins with where you are going.

Part 1: Where You're Going

To attract top producing agents to your brokerage, your brokerage's story must begin with the destination. Most people want opportunities to grow in their careers, so you need to be able to articulate exactly where your brokerage is going in order to excite them.

The secret to being an effective recruiter is to think of your role as being that of a train conductor and your brokerage is the train. You are pulling into the station to pick up passengers. The people standing on the platform have just one question: *Where is this train going?*

The conductor only wants to pick up the passengers that have the desire to go to the specific destination that the train is going to. If the conductor picks up the wrong passengers, chaos and disruption will ensue. The same is true with your brokerage. You only want to bring on the agents that share the common objective that you and your brokerage stand to achieve.

Your objective as the recruiter for your brokerage is to spark enough curiosity with prospective agents that they wonder or better yet ask you: "Where is your brokerage going in five years?" and invite only the agents who are interested in going to that destination to learn more about the journey.

Examples: National Brokerage Destinations

- **Keller Williams Realty:** To be the real estate company of choice for agents and their customers.
- **RE/MAX International:** To be the worldwide real estate leader.
- **Coldwell Banker Real Estate:** To provide our clients the very best customer service in all aspects of residential real estate.

Part 2: Identify the Villain

There are no good stories without a hero and there are no heroes without villains. To create a powerful story for your brokerage that will attract producing agents, you need a villain.

The truth is we are all more likely to avoid pain than we are to move towards pleasure. This is also true when recruiting. Agents are more likely to change brokerages to avoid experiencing loss, pain, disappointment, and embarrassment than they are to save money, gain awards, or even sell more houses.

This is a controversial topic because we are taught not to disparage others, but the villain doesn't need to be a direct competitor. It can be a change in the industry, like technology, market conditions, or consumer preferences. Or it can be something that is directly affecting your neighborhood like gentrification or lack of affordable housing.

Identify a villain for your story, something that your brokerage is fighting against. You will find that when you mobilize around a cause you will attract passionate agents that also care about your cause.

Examples: The Villain with Brokerages

Baird and Warner's Villain: Homelessness
"[Baird and Warner's] **Good Will Network,** is powered by automatic contributions that add $10 to the fund for each real estate transaction..."

Redfin's Villain: Salespeople
"...designed from the ground up, using technology and totally different values, to put customers first. So, we joined forces with agents who wanted to be customer advocates, not salesmen."

RE/MAX's Villain: Working Alone
"At RE/MAX, you're in business for yourself, but not by yourself."

Part 3: Why They Should Follow You

Make no mistake, productive agents can pretty much choose any brokerage they want. So why should they invest the time and energy to move their business to you and your office? Why are you the right choice to get them to the destination that they so deeply desire and how can you help them overcome the villain?

The answer is quite simple because your brokerage was created specifically to achieve this specific objective. Like the train and tracks built to take the passengers swiftly from one destination to the next, your brokerage was painstakingly engineered to achieve this specific mission.

Like Martin Luther King Jr., you too have a dream that one day your brokerage will overcome the tyranny and oppression of the villain that is preventing the happiness and greater good that you wish to see in the world.

I'm sure it sounds a little "over the top" to you, but if you don't have this much conviction and passion for what you are doing you won't achieve the success you desire. Your passion for the outcome is exactly what will attract the right agents to help you fulfill your objective.

Part 4: What They Will Gain

Agents who are considering your real estate brokerage must have a clear vision of what they will gain when they join your brokerage. This is greater than just features and benefits like a better website or nicer marketing. It is the result they want to see for themselves, the brokerage they affiliate with, or their community.

If the agents are in alignment with your brokerage, what they will gain will be the same or similar to what your brokerage will gain when it achieves its objective. This could be achieving the mission, overcoming the villain, or both.

If your brokerage exists to achieve #1 in market share in your community and your villain is a lack of affordable housing, then your agents will gain the satisfaction of being part of a mission greater than themselves and the acknowledgment of being someone who is making a difference in their community by supporting efforts to provide more housing options.

Part 5: Why They Need to Get Started Now

To attract producing agents to your brokerage you must have excitement, passion, and urgency. Urgency creates momentum and momentum, in turn, attracts more productive agents. This is the fuel that grows every successful company.

Just understand that there is a difference between pressure and urgency. Pressure is an external force to do something. Urgency is something that requires immediate attention or action from an internal motivation.

The urgency is that of the impact that your brokerage will make on your clients, community, or industry. The agents you are recruiting will feel that they can begin making an immediate impact by making a brokerage change today. That the sooner they make the change, the sooner they will see the change that they want to see in their world.

The Bottom Line

When you are clear about why your brokerage exists and how it can serve a greater good you will be able to craft a powerful story that attracts producing agents.

The telltale sign of an outstanding story is few objections from agents that align with your vision. They will be inspired, excited, and passionate about being part of something greater and if they are not a fit, they will leave with a clear picture of what your brokerage is about. They may even refer agents to you that desire what you offer.

15

DESIGN A SUCCESSFUL RECRUITING PLAN

It was 2003 when I left my sales position at RE/MAX to partner with another agent to start a boutique real estate brokerage in Denver, Colorado. We were both top producing agents so building a real estate brokerage should have been easy for us… or so we thought.

We believed that agents would join us because we were influential. We thought if we opened a brokerage, they would all contact us for the chance to work with us. Well, they didn't. And after four years we had roughly the same 10 agents that we had the day we opened our brokerage.

In one meeting, my partner said to me *"We need to recruit more agents."* I responded with *"How do we do that?"* He said, *"We call them... I guess?"* *"What would I say?"* I thought to myself.

We were obviously in over our heads. I knew at that moment, I had to learn how to recruit. Since that day nearly twenty years ago, I have received multiple awards for recruiting, as well as national recognition for building one of the fastest-growing real estate brokerages in the state of Colorado.

What I have learned is that being a great agent or running an outstanding team or brokerage does not in itself attract agents. You must have a great offering, a powerful story, and a defined recruiting plan. Luckily, you will if you follow the lessons in this book. I'm going to give you my recruiting plan that allowed me to grow my independent brokerage from 6 to over 100 agents in less than two years.

The Right Mindset to Recruit

Think of recruiting as relationship building. The best way to recruit requires you to build relationships by creating trust and showing your agent prospects that you really do care. Doing this ensures that you are attracting the right agents into your organization and increases the chance that they don't leave after you have invested a lot of time and money into them.

The right way to recruit is slow, methodical, and planned out. The plan is to make sure that nothing was overlooked in their decision to change brokerages. This includes the agent and you.

The decision for an agent to change brokerages is likely the second-largest decision they will make next to getting married. We are talking about their career path and their future income here; they are not going to take this lightly so neither should you.

Why a Recruiting Plan is a MUST for Your Brokerage

Many brokerages don't see the value of having a recruiting plan. They believe if they provide good service for their agents the agents they have won't leave and other agents will be attracted to the company. This, unfortunately, is not true.

Sure, some agents will tell other agents and your company will see some growth, but will you attract the agents you want or just the ones that happen to show up? True recruiting is identifying the agents you want and actively marketing and prospecting to them, so they have time to develop trust with you and learn more about your brokerage. This takes both time and intentionality.

Additionally, the hard truth is that over time, all brokerages will lose agents, and you will too. Whether you lose them to the competition or to attrition, the fact is no matter how good you are at supporting your agents, you're going to lose some.

Loss of agents will impact the success of your brokerage. Fewer agents will result in lower potential revenue and reduced revenue means fewer services for your remaining agents. It also begins to create doubt and fear with the remaining agents. This leads to agents being vulnerable to other recruiters, or worse, actively searching for greener pastures by shopping for other brokerages.

A steady flow of new members provides more future revenue, and who isn't looking for that? Therefore, you must have a plan to recruit even if it is only to add a handful of agents each year.

Creating a Recruiting Plan

Now that you have decided if your brokerage needs a brick-and-mortar office, what your splits and fees are and what type of agents you want to work with, you can create your brokerage recruiting plan. The goal of the plan is to accomplish two things: first the number of agents you wish to recruit, and second the timeframe that you wish to recruit them.

Revisiting your budget, look to see how many agents you must have to maintain profitability for a 12-month period. For instance, you may reach profitability in month 6, but you may have known additional expenses that will occur in month 12. This could be something like a rent increase or a new position to hire.

Let's pretend that you are launching a traditional brokerage with a small office, two full-time employees, and an outsourced Transaction Coordinator. After you complete your budget worksheet, you realize that you must have 15 agents to reach 12-months profitability.

In this example, we will assume you already have 3 agents, including yourself. Since your goal is to have the brokerage pay you, we won't count you as one of the agents. Exclude any other agents, like your spouse, that won't be paying split or fees to the brokerage.

So, this leaves you with 2 agents. Therefore, for your brokerage to achieve 12-months profitability you must add 13 more agents.

Your Brokerage's Runway

Next, you must determine your runway. Your runway is the amount of money you are willing to spend until you reach profitability. Looking at the budget worksheet you can see the monthly profit or loss for each month. In the first 6-months to a year of operation, it is likely that your brokerage will lose money. If you don't recruit quickly enough it may lose money for years!

If you are planning to invest $150,000 into your brokerage, expect to spend $50,000 on the deposit, fixtures, furniture, and equipment. You will also have other startup expenses like insurance, licenses, website, etc. Let's budget $15,000 for that. Now it's not a good plan to blow through the remaining money so take an additional $20,000 and set it aside for emergencies.

The $65,000 left over is the money you will use to operate your brokerage until you reach 12-month profitability. This is your runway.

Now, go back to your budget and look to see how many months you can go before your runway runs out. If you have more than enough runway money then your budgeted recruiting numbers are strong enough to get you over the initial start-up hump.

If your runway money runs out before you reach the 12-month profitability, then you will need to recruit faster in order to not run out of runway. Some founders are concerned that it is difficult to recruit when you first open a brokerage. The opposite is actually true, if you follow what I teach in this book, and you are prepared to support agents from the first day you open, you can take advantage of the recruiting sweet spot.

The Recruiting Sweet Spot

There is a sweet spot when you are opening a new brokerage, one where agents in the area are curious and are willing to meet with you to learn more. This is the reason your story is important. The sweet spot will only last for a year or two. After that, your brokerage will become just another brokerage in town. So, to take advantage of the sweet spot you must be proactive and recruit right out the gate.

Now that you know exactly how many agents you MUST recruit to achieve your business plan BEFORE your runway runs out you can begin recruiting.

Where to Begin Recruiting

Begin your recruiting with the type of agents you are already equipped to support. You can always add in other agent types later as you expand your offerings to serve more agent types.

Since I am a teacher at heart, when I opened my independent brokerage in Boulder, Colorado I began with training new and newer agents. I believed that if I could get brand new agents to become successful quickly it would show the mid-level agents that I can help them also.

After accomplishing this I was then able to attract Top Producers and Teams. This successful plan allowed us to become the fourth-largest brokerage in the competitive Boulder real estate market in less than three years.

Let's take a quick look at the different types of agents and what they each need to support them

New Agents

If you are planning on recruiting agents that have sold fewer than three homes in the past year, then you need to be prepared to spend a significant amount of time training them on the basics of real estate. Training more than two or three newer agents at a time can become a full-time job.

If you choose to hire more than a few new agents at a time you will need a designated mentor or trainer and a detailed educational program that includes how they manage a database, do their marketing, give buyer and seller presentations, and how to write and negotiate contracts. Fortunately, we provide these resources on The Close Pro. It is a low-cost membership site for real estate professionals. Learn more at https://courses.theclose.com/bundles/the-close-pro.

Otherwise, their needs will impact your personal real estate production. And trust me when I say, you won't make as much money training new agents as you will just doing a few more sales each year. For this reason, I strongly suggest that if you don't have the resources to train new agents then don't recruit them.

How to Recruit New Agents

There are two types of new agents: pre-licensed and in-school. Pre-licensed are people who are interested in getting their real estate license in the future. In-school are people who are currently in real estate school or that have recently graduated and are interviewing brokerages.

Collect pre-licensed and in-school leads by placing ads on employment websites like Indeed, Career Builder, and Craigslist. Your ad headline will read something like: "Successful Brokerage Needs More Agents. We Will Help You Get Licensed."

When they contact you, they will have general questions about starting a real estate career.

Answer their questions then direct them to a local real estate licensing school or an online school. The most important thing is to keep in touch with them throughout the process, so they are sure to interview you once they receive their license.

If you are familiar with the real estate school material, you can even have a once-a-week study hall in your office where pre-licensees can ask you questions and get in the habit of coming to your office.

You can find the in-school leads by contacting your local real estate schools and asking if you can present the benefits of your brokerage. They will usually ask you to bring lunches or snacks for the students in exchange for a 15-minute presentation. Some universities that offer a degree in real estate can also be a great resource

Mid-Level Agents

These are the agents that fall between 8-20 transactions each year. They have some basic needs, like a good website, a great CRM, lead generation support, and a sense of community. Overall, they are the easiest agents to manage and also the easiest to overlook.

Since this group is so often forgotten by most brokerages, they are also the most common to recruit and be recruited from your brokerage.

For this reason, you must create a strong sense of community in your brokerage. You can do this by having regular team meetings, group lead generation activities, and mobilizing around a common vision or cause. This could be increasing the market share of your organization or even donating to a charity you all care about.

I will share in detail in the next chapter how to find and recruit these agents.

Top Producers

I categorize Top Producers as agents who sell more than 30 homes a year. They are often considered to be unreasonable or demanding. Since most companies want Top Producers, they are usually able to get their demands met by someone. Does this make them demanding or just knowing what they can ask for?

The demands of Top Producers may vary greatly but they mainly have three things that they are seeking: more opportunities, a better compensation plan, or recognition for their efforts.

The Needs of a Top Producing Real Estate Agent

Opportunities

For Top Producers, opportunities come in many different forms. It can be the opportunity for a leadership role in an organization or even just an impressive title they can put on their business card. For others, it is the ability to learn something new or have access to better training or mentors.

Recognition

Some Top Producers thrive on the approval of others (I too am guilty of this). Believe it or not, there are many companies that are not good at giving credit where credit is due.

Top Producers typically invest more time and more of their own money into their businesses than other agents. All this helps your brokerage grow your brand. Therefore, they deserve special treatment, don't they? I think so.

It's not that they need you to kiss their butt; they just need to know that you appreciate having them in your organization. You can do this by creating unique experiences that only they are invited to. This can include taking them to sporting events and introducing them to influential people. I once took my top agents to see Tony Robbins in Palm Springs. They still talk about this trip, 14 years later.

Compensation

The third recruiting need a Top Producer seeks is a better compensation plan. Many Top Producers selected their brokerage and negotiated their compensation plan long before they became a Top Producer. Now they find themselves paying an unfair share of their commissions to their brokerage and they are seeking a better deal.

DO NOT... I repeat do not, change your compensation model to accommodate a Top Producer. This will lead to animosity among your other agents if they feel you gave them a better deal than what they are receiving. This leads them to resent the Top Producer. Resentment can divide your brokerage.

If you want to attract this type of agent, then start from the beginning to build your brokerage model's compensation plan to attract financially-conscious Top Producers.

If you already operate a brokerage with an established compensation model, consider paying an upfront joining bonus in lieu of modifying your compensation model. This allows them the benefit of reducing their overhead and it doesn't disrupt your financial model. I have found that even the agents within my brokerages preferred me to pay a Top Producer to join rather than for me to offer lower splits and fees.

Recruiting Solves Your Brokerage's Problems

In late 2009 I took over the CEO position of a failing Keller Williams franchise office in Denver Colorado. A few years earlier, the office was over 200 agents strong and making over half a million dollars in annual profit. When a brokerage starts to make "real" money, the common response is to spend it.

After working hard and sacrificing all the little things for years before seeing even a dollar in annual profit, it's easy to understand why one would want to spend some of the hard-earned profits. The previous owners of this franchise were no different and leased a new expensive office, rented multiple costly copy machines, and purchased all new furniture.

By June of 2009, the Great Recession was well underway and the housing market was falling like Newton's Apple. Agents were leaving the business to find hourly jobs and those of us that remained found our income cut in half.

The drop in agent count and reduced commission incomes trickled down to the brokerage office's bottom line. Within just a few months the once successful office was now losing tens of thousands a month. Financially strapped, the owners were forced to sell the office for pennies on the dollar.

The new owner was able to reduce the office size and renegotiate the lease. He also returned the fancy copy machines and purchased a basic used unit, and sold the access furniture for some quick cash. He also hired me.

When I took over the CEO position the brokerage showed 110 agents on the roster, but when we audited the roster we found that there were really only 75 agents left. This meant that despite the cost-cutting efforts the brokerage was still losing money. There was only one solution… Recruit more agents!

I sat down with the staff to do the math on how many agents we would need to recruit to return the office to the successful, profitable brokerage it one was. We projected we would need to get to a minimum of 100 agents for the brokerage to achieve our goal of month-over-month profitability and 140 agents for the brokerage to reach the annual profit goals.

We also realized that due to the recession, we were likely going to lose some more of the 75 remaining agents, and not all the new agents we hired would stay at our brokerage or survive the recession over a year. Therefore we estimated that we would need to recruit 100 more agents to net 140 after a year.

With our backs against a wall, we got to work. Our goal was to interview ten and hire two agents each week. Once added to the team, we would teach them how to find and work with homeowners who were in financial distress. We became known in our city as "The Short-Sale" brokerage.

Within a few short months, we reached a break-even point, then month over month profitability, and finally we broke 140 agents. By the end of the year, we had recruited 116 agents to a brokerage with a small office and a used copy machine!

In a real estate brokerage, productive agents will increase your revenue. Depending on your financial model each agent can add $200-$1000 a month to your bottom line! Whatever the challenge that you face with your brokerage, more income isn't likely to make the problem worse.

For us, recruiting was the solution to all of our brokerage problems. It became our mantra… Do you need a new copy machine? Recruit four producing agents and you can afford a new copy machine. Want to upgrade your audio and visual system? Recruit two more producing agents. Do your agents want an in-house Transaction Coordinator? Ask them to help you add ten producing agents.

The Bottom Line

Recruiting is the lifeblood of a real estate brokerage. In the next chapter, we will review the strategies I developed to help me recruit over 100 agents a year to my brokerages.

Knowing the type of agents you want to attract, how many agents you need to achieve your goals, and the strategies to recruit them completes your recruiting plan. So take the time to write out your decisions and commitments so your brokerage can exceed its goals.

16

THE 10 BEST RECRUITING STRATEGIES
[PLUS SCRIPTS AND AD]

If you wish to be successful with your real estate brokerage then recruiting talented people must become a top priority for you. However, it can be difficult to manage the day-to-day operations and find time for recruiting.

For over 20-years, I have built and operated multi-million dollar brokerages and in doing so I have personally recruited well over 600 agents. My secret isn't that I am an amazing recruiter. There are many people much better than me. The truth is that I have learned and developed recruiting strategies that work! In this chapter, I will share my 10 best recruiting strategies that will make your task of recruiting wildly successful.

1. Real Estate Schools

If you're looking for new up-in-coming agents for your brokerage then real estate schools can be an outstanding resource. However real estate schools can be full of a lot of people who are not looking for a real estate career. Real estate investors, part-time income seekers, and hobbyists also seek out getting a real estate license.

The key to sifting through the wanna-bees and not-gonna-bees to find the future superstars is having clear guidelines of who you are looking for. A "Talent Wanted" description of: full-time, coachable, learning-based, growth-minded, wants to earn over $100k a year, will narrow the calling to the few motivated students that will hear the calling.

Begin by calling the local "In-Class" schools and request giving a presentation in exchange for lunch. Don't be a cheapskate and bring $5 pizzas. The lunch you bring will represent the standards for your brokerage or team. Who wants to work for a company that isn't willing to spring for a decent meal?

Some online schools will provide student lists… for a fee of course! Use the script from the advertising section to help you craft an email to attract the best response from your emails.

2. Agent Referrals

Who better to find the right agents for your brokerage than the agents that you are already working with. It is easy to think that your agents will refer their friends already, but that simply isn't the case.

Agents are busy and referring other agents to your brokerage just isn't top-of-mind for them. You must ask to remind them of your need or desire to grow the team. Begin by reminding them why it is a benefit to them for the brokerage to grow. I say something like this, "More agents means more signs… and more signs means more customer recognition. You want your customers to recognize the brand, right? Then we need to hire more agents!"

Then I say, "I appreciate (Insert a value they possess) about you, can you think of another agent that is (repeat the value) like yourself, that would be a good fit for (brokerage)?"

After they give you a name, then ask, *"May I use your name when I call them today?"*

It is also beneficial to incentivize agents for referring other agents to the brokerage. It doesn't have to be a large incentive. A month's free office bill or $200 after the referred agent closes their first transaction with the company.

Contests are also a great way to keep referring top-of-mind for the agents. Give away a $100 gift card to any agent who refers the most agents to the brokerage by the end of the month.

3. Vendor Referrals

An agent referral from a trusted vendor is a powerful lead when you are recruiting for a real estate brokerage. The trusted vendors I'm speaking of include but are not limited to Mortgage Lenders, Title

Representatives, Home Inspectors, Home Warranty Providers, and Property Insurance Agents that you know and trust.

These vendors want access to your agents and to be promoted within your brokerage, so in turn, ask them to support your recruiting goals.

The next time a vendor approaches you to sponsor a team meeting or ask you to lunch, flip the script! Share with them that you are happy to discuss a mutual referral relationship. Set a meeting with them to share your brokerage or team's vision, values, and recruiting goals.

Ask them if they are willing to discuss the opportunities to work on your brokerage with other agents that may be unhappy where they're at and looking for a change.

4. Networking

Instead of attending REALTOR events for the purpose of learning about the latest listings, go for the opportunity to network with agents. Networking is a great way to find the right agents for your real estate brokerage.

Your local Association of REALTORS hosts educational, social, and marketing events. While directly recruiting from the events is not permitted, it is a great opportunity to network with your fellow REALTORS.

When you meet an agent that you want to join your brokerage you can invite the agent to a more formal discussion outside the REALTOR event. You can do this with the Four-Step Recruiting Questions.

The Four-Step Recruiting Questions

STEP 1
"What was your goal this year?"
They will typically say a number between 24-36 homes.

STEP 2
"Are you on track to reach your goal?"

The average REALTOR sells 10-12 homes a year, so they are most likely behind on their goal.

STEP 3

"What do you believe is preventing you from reaching your goal?"

Most agents will say that marketing, leads, or lack of lead generation is preventing them from reaching their goals.

STEP 4

"Would you like to meet to discuss how you can get back on track?"

Set a meeting at your office to discuss how your brokerage can help them achieve their goals.

5. Top Producer Mastermind

Top Producers love high-level conversations with other Top Producers. So if you are wanting to attract Top Producing agents to your brokerage then take note.

Begin by selecting an interesting topic like the challenges of having a lack of inventory or social media best practices. Invite one Top Producer from each real estate brokerage brand. Your goal is to keep it small; 6-8 people including yourself. When you call, tell them that you are hosting a Top Producer—only mastermind and you would like it if they could attend to represent their brokerage.

Host the Mastermind at a local (high-end) restaurant. Ask for a private room if they have one available. Plan the event for late morning or after lunch so you are not expected to pay for meals or alcohol.

At the meeting, you MUST take the lead and guide meaningful conversations about the topic. Have someone agree to take notes that you will share with everyone after the event.

Listen for opportunities for you to follow up with each agent. If they are having challenges with social media then let them know that you are happy to sit down with them one-on-one to help them to create a social media marketing plan.

Before you are finished, don't forget to schedule the next Mastermind and topic for the next month!

6. Coop Agent

Coop agents have a unique perspective since they recently had a transaction with your brokerage. If everything went as planned they are sure to have a positive response to you inquiring about the transaction. If things went poorly they will be impressed that you are calling for their honest feedback.

Coop Agent Script

"Hello, this is (name). You recently had a transaction with (your agent) on (address). I am calling today to ask how the transaction went. We strive to be the most professional agents in the industry."

"May I ask, is there anything that we or our agent could have improved upon to make this transaction better?"

The key here is to listen to their honest feedback. No matter what they say, don't get defensive. Once you feel you have received the feedback from the transaction, pivot the conversation to their business by asking them The Four-Step Recruiting Questions discussed previously.

7. Social Media

Some agents are very active on social media sites like Facebook, Instagram, Pinterest, and TikTok. This gives you a great opportunity to start a friendship online and invite them to meet in person later.

Start by selecting 10-20 agents you are interested in getting to know better. Connect with and follow each agent. On Facebook, you can create a Custom Friends List to keep them organized.

The secret is to be observant of their activities. Like and comment on their posts, so they begin to familiarize themselves with you. Once you feel comfortable that they know who you are, you can connect with them via Instant Messenger (IM) or Direct Message (DM).

Post Response Scripts

When you see an agent running an making a creative post or running a listing Ad, send them a message;

Creative Post
"Hey (name), I saw your post on FB, and I was impressed…. I love creative social media marketing ideas. I have some creative marketing ideas of my own that I would be happy to share with you. Would you be interested in meeting to discuss?"

Listing Ad
"Hey (name), I saw your ad for your listing on FB. It's a great listing! Do you sell most of your homes in (area)?"
After they reply, *"Yes"*.
Say, *"Are you interested in getting more listings in (area)? We are looking to invest in a few agents to help them grow their business in (area). Would you be interested in meeting to discuss?"*

8. Classes, Events, and Seminars

A tried and true way to recruit agents to your real estate brokerage is to hold classes, events, and seminars. These give agents an opportunity to learn about your knowledge, culture, and values while providing important training to the agents on your team or brokerage.

Reserve a space in your building or in a vendor's offsite location. It doesn't need to be too large, just big enough to hold 20-30 people. This will be large enough to have 10-15 agents from your brokerage and 10-15 guests. Ask a vendor to provide snacks and water.

Next, select a topic that will interest the agents you wish to attract to your brokerage. While Continuing Education classes are important, I have found that the dry topics don't draw the type of agents I want for my brokerage. Here is a shortlist of "Hot Topics" that will attract motivated agents that want to grow their real estate businesses:

Hot Topics for Classes, Events, and Seminars

1. Social Media Marketing Plan
2. Facebook Ad Strategies
3. Real Estate Investment Strategies
4. Real Estate Business Planning
5. Top Producer Panelist Discussions

Prepare to talk on one of the Hot Topics for 45-90 minutes. It is best practice for you to present the information. This will make you the expert and the guests more likely to want to meet and speak with you after.

The best way to organize the information is the What-Why Presentation Format.

What-Why Presentation Format:

1. What is the challenge or problem?
2. Why is it important to them?
3. What will happen if they don't address it?
4. Why is it a difficult problem to solve?
5. What results have you got with solving the problem?

Notice in the What-Why Presentation Format we don't share with them "HOW" to solve the problem. This is because the solution isn't that easy or they would have resolved it already, and they are not likely to fix the problem on their own. They need your help.

Instead of giving them the solution... give them a reason to meet with you!

Here is what you say, *"We don't have time to cover the entire solution today, so if you are interested in solving (challenge or problem)* I'm happy to meet with you one-on-one. I have my calendar here and I will schedule a time with you today."

9. Open Houses

As a recruiter for your brokerage you probably wish there was a place to go every week to meet productive agents. Well, there are... open houses! Attending open houses and broker opens each weekend is one of the easiest and most efficient ways to build relationships with active and producing agents.

Follow my simple plan and script to meet agents at open houses.

Open House Recruiting Procedure and Script

1. Each week do a quick search for upcoming open houses or broker opens in your area.
2. Send the agent an email letting them know that you will be stopping by to preview the listing. This will make your introduction easier when you're at the open house. Additionally, if the open house is busy, it gives you a reason to follow up later to give them feedback.
3. Map the open houses to save drive time.
4. Spending 10-15 minutes in each open house, just long enough to preview the property and have a quick conversation with the agent.
5. After a short friendly conversation with the agent, ask them the following questions:
   "Do you sell most of your homes in (area)?"

   After they reply, "Yes".

   Say, *"Are you interested in getting more listings in (area)? We are looking to invest in a few agents to help them grow their business in (area). Would you be interested in meeting to discuss?"*

10. Help Wanted Ads

A simple and efficient method of finding real estate agents for your brokerage is placing Help Wanted Ads. Websites like ZipRecruiter, Career Builder, and Indeed are all outstanding sources for finding talented people looking to make a career change. What I like about websites like this is that you can promote your ad to keep it at the top of the prospects' search.

Craigslist, on the other hand, is a lower cost than the other websites but your ad will quickly fall to the bottom of the help wanted ads. Therefore you will need to post your ad more frequently to keep it top of mind. I have found that posting twice a week, on Monday and Thursday, generates the best results.

Here is a copy of my top-performing help wanted recruiting ad:

Help Wanted Agent Recruiting Ad

We Are Hiring Real Estate Agents! We Offer Real Estate License School and Sales Training!

(Company) is a gathering place for (Area's) best talent. This first-rate market center features a state-of-the-art training room and a friendly atmosphere that is recognizable the moment you enter. As one of the fastest-growing real estate offices in one of the fastest-growing marketplaces, (Company) is a hot spot for agents looking to grow their careers rapidly and organically.

We are hiring because our sales are up a BLISTERING 200% over last year! We need help! Hardworking, motivated, Agents that want a great opportunity!

- Earn a six-figure income
- Work your own hours
- Fun work atmosphere
- Free training and support
- No previous experience necessary
- In-class and online Real Estate School
- Low cost to start!

Already In Real Estate School? Please interview with us!

We're looking for people who are:

- Positive and friendly
- Learning-Based
- Wanting to increase their business
- Willing to work hard

What's next?
When you're ready to begin the journey, fill out the contact form found on our website.

The Bottom Line

Recruiting is an essential practice for any real estate brokerage and having a clear plan on how you're going to attract the right people is the first step. The 10 recruiting strategies are proven ways for you to grow your brokerage. It's just up to you now!

17

BONUS SECTION
THE COMPLETE GUIDE TO RECRUITING PRODUCING AGENTS
(+ SCRIPTS & OBJECTION HANDLERS)

Just like all sales, your success in recruiting agents to your brokerage is dependent upon your ability to identify the right leads, find their contact information, and build relationships with them. Recruiting mid-level and top producing agents is a completely different process than recruiting new and newer agents. You will need to source both the agent's contact information and current sales performance.

Knowing how to find agents' production and contact information is gold when it comes to recruiting agents for your brokerage. However, to be successful at this you don't need to have their exact production. Stay focused on the production of only the agents in the areas you want to recruit from, not the entire MLS.

How to Find the Producing Agent's Production & Contact Information

If you would like to recruit producing agents to your brokerage, you must get an idea of the agents' production in your area and their contact information. This can be done manually through your MLS or in just a few clicks with recruiting software like BrokerMetrics. BrokerMetrics starts at $200 a month for the basic tools. In addition to agent production and contact information BrokerMetrics can also provide market share and trend reports.

In this example, I am using the Matrix MLS system but most MLS Systems offer the same ability to search closed transactions for market analysis reasons. If exporting and manipulating excel files are not your cup of tea then you can farm this out to an admin or virtual assistant.

Begin with a search of recently sold homes in the past six months. Limit the search to a 1–2-mile radius around your office or the territory you would like to expand your brokerage. This will ensure you have agents that are doing business in your area.

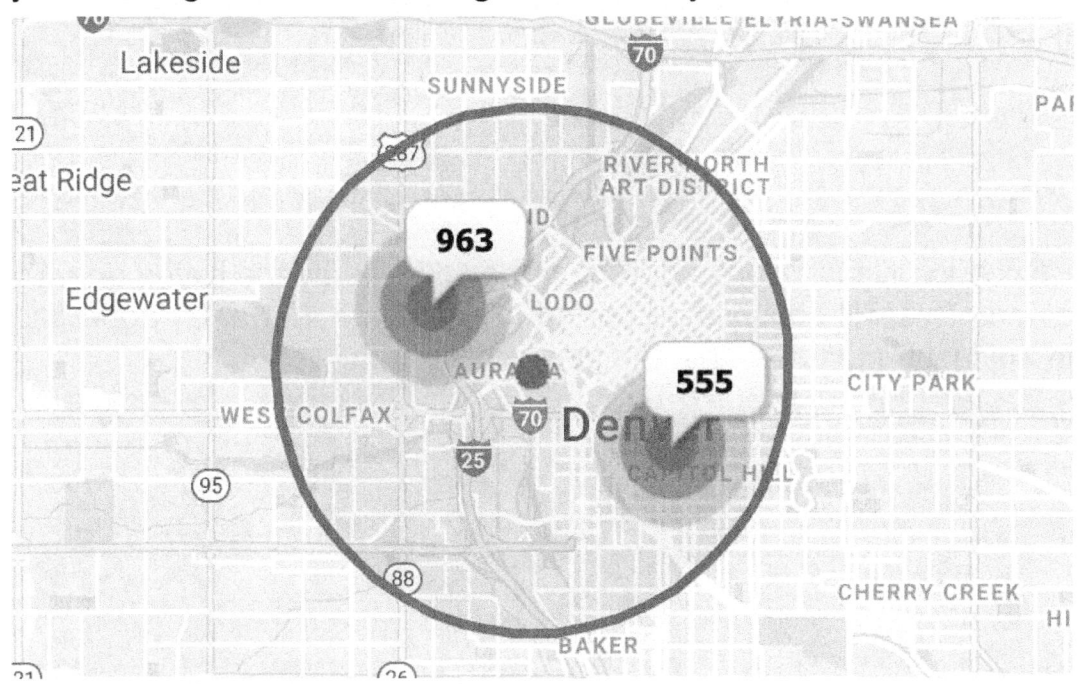

Next, export the full search information into a CSV file. Be sure that the export includes both the Listing Agent and Buyer's Agent's contact information.

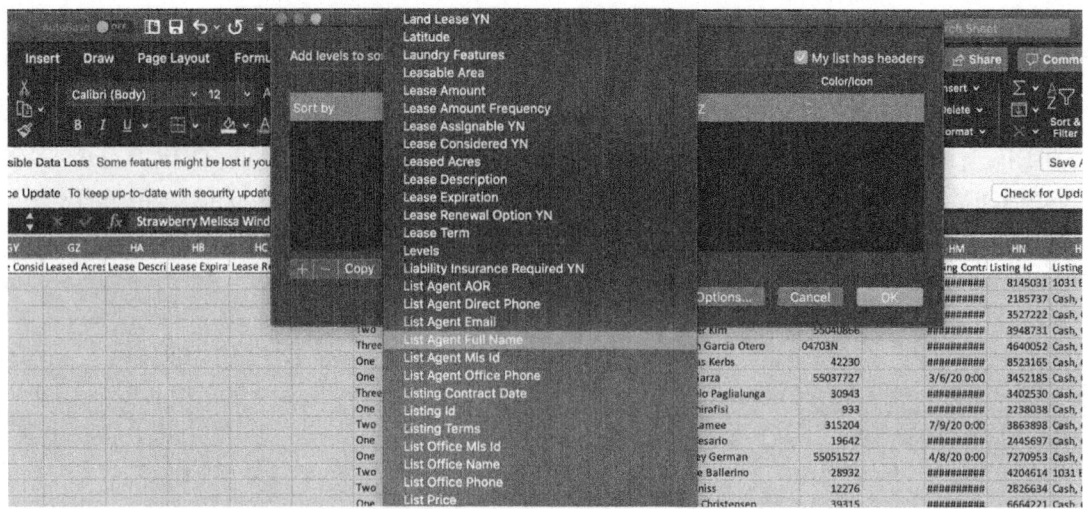

Once the file is downloaded, sort the CSV file by the listing agent's name. This will consolidate all the transactions that each agent did in the last 6-months within the geographic area.

In this example, we can see that Alissa Edwards has closed five sales in the area in just the past six months. To me, this suggests that Alissa likely specializes in the area and may be a good recruiting prospect. Notice her contact information is also listed (in yellow).

In this simple search of 1500 closed transactions, I was able to identify over 100 producing agents who sold over two transactions in the past six months, within two miles of my office. These agents would be excellent leads for recruitment.

[Spreadsheet screenshot showing columns BR through CC with buyer agent data including columns for Buyer Agency %, Buyer Agent name, phone, email, Buyer Agent Full Name, Buyer Financing, Buyer Office, and phone numbers. Rows include agents such as Aaron Graybill, Aaron Luttrell, Aaron Stailey, Aaron Weinzapfel, Abell To Sell, Adam Andrus, Adam Haligas, Adam Hilliard, Adam Waggoner, Adelia Redalen, Adrian Dedering, Adrian Phan, and Adriana Zuleta.]

Next, repeat the sorting using the buyer agent's name. This will give you a hefty list of agents who are working with buyers in your territory. Personally, to further narrow the list, I would eliminate agents who have only closed one transaction from the list.

After this process, you now have a list of producing agents in your area. Now all you have to do is have a good reason to contact them.

The Best Scripts for Recruiting Agents

If you only learn one thing about recruiting scripts from this, it should be this: **The best script is the true script.**

What I mean by this is don't say you are something that you are not. For instance, don't say that you are a training organization if you don't have training. Don't say that you will provide excellent service if you don't have the staff to support them. Get very clear about who you are and are not.

If you are a boutique brokerage that wants to build your brand, then make that clear in your script. Sure, this script won't appeal to a top producer who is interested in growing their own personal brand but it will resonate with a mid-level agent who wants to be part of something and isn't concerned about being the out front.

Your goal should not be to get appointments with all the agents, your goal is to meet with the right agents.

Think of your script as a way to weed out the agents that don't fit, not simply get appointments. I would much rather have three appointments a week with people who are looking for what I am offering than having 10 appointments with people who have no interest, need, or willingness to pay for what my organization offers.

With this in mind, here are the four most effective scripts I have used to recruit producing agents to my brokerages.

The Best "New to the Area" Recruiting Script

This script is best used to recruit producing agents to your brokerage if you or your organization is new to the area or is looking to expand into a new territory.

Once you've gathered a list of recruiting leads using my process above, use the following script to contact them.

(The secret of this script is to start with curiosity in your voice)

Hello (Name), this is _(Your Name)_ with___(Brokerage)___.

I see that you have recently sold _(#)_ homes in the _(Specific Location)_ area.

Do you specialize in _(Specific Location)_?

Are you looking to do more business in _(Specific Location)_?

(If they say YES… Shift your voice to excitement!)

Great! The reason for my call today is because we recently opened a new office in _(Location)__and we are looking to invest in a few agents to help them grow their business in _(Specific Location)_.

Would you like to have a conversation about that?

Are you available_____at_:_?

Many recruiters would scoff and say that this script is too direct. This is because many companies reward recruiters for the number of appointments they set and not the quality of the lead or appointment. The key to recruiting success is to find the right candidates to join your organization not to get appointments with everyone with a real estate license.

Another concern I hear with this script is with the word *invest*. Recruiters say things like *"I don't have money to give them."* or *"We don't BUY agents."*

My response to this is, the word invest can also mean investing your time in mentoring them, investing by providing them your extra leads, or investing in them financially. However you choose to invest is up to you. If you don't plan on investing in agents in some way you are going to have a hard time attracting talented agents and retaining the agents you have.

The Most Effective Mid-Level Agent Recruiting Script

Use this script for agents that market specifically to a community, neighborhood, or town. Begin by paying attention to their advertising on Facebook, newspapers, and listing signs. When you see they are marketing a unique message or a new listing contact them with the following script.

Hello (Name), this is _(Your Name)_ with _(Brokerage)_.

The reason I am calling is I saw your _(Advertisement)_ and I was impressed by _(the message, quality, or professionalism)_.

I see you have a listing in ___(Specific Location)___. Do you sell most of your homes in _(Specific Location)_?

Are you interested in getting more Listings in _(Specific Location)_?

We are also looking to grow in _(Specific Location) and we are looking to invest in a few agents to help them grow their business in _(Specific Location)_.

Would you like to have a conversation about that?

Are you available_____ at _:_?

This is one of my favorite recruiting scripts because it works on Facebook IM, texting, and even on Slydial. As long as you are honest and transparent about their ad or marketing. If you are just spraying this message to all the agents, they will quickly figure out it is insincere. If agents think you truly don't care about them, they will dismiss you in the future.

The Best Events and Seminar Agent Recruiting Script

Holding events and seminars is an outstanding way to attract agents that are learning-based. These agents will likely be newer in the business and mid-level seasoned agents looking for new ideas on how to generate more business.

Choose a trendy lead generation topic that you or a panel can speak about for 60-90 minutes. It is the BEST PRACTICE for you to present the information or host the panel. This will position you as the expert… and everyone wants to know the expert.

Here is a shortlist of the trendiest real estate topics right now.

Top Trendy Real Estate Topics:

1. Instagram and TikTok Strategies
2. Paid Facebook Ad Strategies
3. Real Estate Business Planning
4. Virtual Real Estate Showings and Transactions
5. Using Cryptocurrency to Close Transactions

Keep it a small event or seminar for only 5-25 agents. For a location, you can use either a conference room in your building or a vendor's (mortgage or title company's) neutral location.

Just don't hold it in your office. Agents will be intimidated to come into the lion's den.

Next, invite agents to your event.

Here is the exact script I use to get real estate agents to my events.

Hello (Name), this is _(Your Name)_ with_(Brokerage)_.

The reason for my call is _(Vendor) and ___(Brokerage)__ are holding an event for real estate agents called:____(Title of the Event or Subject)_ where we will go into detail about:

1. How to_____(get a specific result)_____
2. How to_____(get a specific result)_____
3. How to_____(get a specific result)_____

Are you interested in attending?

(If they are interested, they will ask what day and time the event is)

The event is on __(date and time)__ and is at __(Location)__ and is limited to _(5-25)_ agents. Can I mark you down to hold your seat?

The secret to successfully recruiting with events and seminars is converting the conversation from the event to why they should take the time to meet with you one on one. Think of your event as a lead magnet on your website. You need to offer something they want, but your end goal should be to convert them into recruitment leads.

Think about it this way. The event is mainly for you to build trust with them. Trust is built through familiarity. They see you at an event, then later meet you at an association meeting, and then you call them to set a meeting. Then they are more likely to listen to your message without dismissing you. This is because you are already familiar with them. Yet, the event by itself will not get you a meeting.

The Columbo Script

If you want a producing agent to meet with you, you must give them a good reason to. I call this the "Columbo Script." If you are a little older you may remember the TV series, Columbo, where the detective Columbo would say *"Just one more thing"* before revealing the secret to solving the mystery.

At some point during the event, ideally in the middle, you will tell the agents transparently why you are hosting the event.

"I am hosting this event because I am looking to grow my brokerage in _(Location)_ and wish to _(The result you want to achieve; grow market share, etc.) I am looking for agents that are looking to _(The result you want)_ too."

Without going any further say...

"Just one more thing... If you want to be more effective with __(The Event Topic)_ then meet with me and I will provide you with__(Something of value, like a script, an example, a worksheet, etc.) This will help you achieve _(The Event Results)_ faster."

Zoom Events and Seminars

The event and seminar script also works very well for Zoom events. The best practice is to keep the attendance limited to 10-15 agents and ask the attendees to turn their cameras on to ensure their participation.

Remember your #1 goal is to build trust, not to close them on the Zoom event.

The Best Top Producer Recruiting Script Ever!

Ask any real estate recruiter and they will tell you their greatest challenge is recruiting Top Producers. This is because the other recruiting techniques often don't resonate with someone who has their own processes and systems, has a great personal brand, and already has tons of business.

As we discussed earlier in this chapter, Top Producers are attracted to three things: opportunities, recognition, and/or compensation. Therefore, the secret to recruiting Top Producing agents is to treat them differently than the other agents... because they've earned it.

Be direct, clear, and concise. Don't be shy, either pick up the phone or walk into their office. An email, text, or IM doesn't work for this script.

Hello (Name), this is _(Your Name)_ with__(Brokerage)__. You may not have heard of me but I surely have heard of you.

The reason I am calling you today is to invite you to an opportunity that is only available to a select few Top Producing agents like yourself. Are you available_(Day)_ at _(Time)_? (Pause)

(They will ask what the opportunity is)

This is an exclusive opportunity that is only available to a select few Top Producing agents, like yourself, and due to privacy, I can't share with you specifically what it is. What I can tell you is that: it is limited, it is in real estate, and it is a once-in-a-lifetime opportunity. Can you make it on_(Day)_ at _(Time)_?

(At this point they will reluctantly agree to meet or politely reject your offer)

I am sure, just like them, you are wondering what the opportunity is right?

Well, that is completely up to you to decide. The opportunity could be the chance to meet someone influential in the industry, or the chance to have an amazing experience to show you recognize them, or the opportunity to join your organization at the ground floor before it goes to the next level. Whatever the opportunity is, this script will help you get them there.

The Best Recruiting Objection Handlers

No guide to recruiting agents can be complete without addressing the common objections real estate agents have when being recruited. Remember when recruiting you are playing the long game. You are likely going to be in business for more than just a few years so it is important not to burn relationships by trying to close them when they're not ready, or by being too pushy.

Therefore, these objection handlers are to be used when speaking to an agent that you believe is a fit for your brokerage. If you overuse objection handlers you can come across as insensitive to them and they may not want to meet with you in the future.

That being said, here is a list of the most common real estate recruiting objections and how to handle them.

Most Common Real Estate Recruiting Objections

I don't want to move at this time. (Too Busy...)

> *Honestly, as a successful, busy agent, there is never a good time to make a move. The good news is we can help make the transition easier. The sooner you can make the move the sooner we can implement your new plan.*

I am loyal to my Broker/Office. (I'm happy where I am at...)

> *I respect the fact that you are loyal. In fact, that is exactly why I am interested in working with you. Let's be honest, if you were getting the support you need, would you even be talking with me right now?*

I don't want to leave my friends.

> *If I could demonstrate that we are not only a good fit for you, but it would also be good for them, how would you feel about bringing them by to meet me?*

I don't want to deal with the hassle of changing companies.

> *I understand completely. Many busy agents that have already joined us had the same concern. That is why we help you with the transition. Let's go over a transition plan.*

I don't know how I can support myself without leads. (My broker gives me leads)

What percentage of your leads are coming from your company? What is your split on those leads? (Figure out your commission) If I can show you how to generate more income without having to be handed leads would you look at joining my company?

Your company costs more than I pay now. (I don't want to pay _____...)

To make more money you must increase revenue, not simply cut your expenses. It doesn't matter if your expenses are $0 if you are not generating enough income. What I will show you how to do is make enough money that the additional expense won't matter.

I think I could sell more homes if I were with a better-known company.

You're right! NAR statistics show that consumers choose an agent by the company only 5% of the time. So, if we can show you how to increase your business by 20% would you be okay with a lesser-known company?

The Bottom Line

Ultimately, your success in recruiting agents lies in your ability to clearly communicate to the right type of agents the services your brokerage provides.

All brokerages will lose agents over time. You must have a plan to recruit agents in order to grow or even just maintain your market share.

Your script is the first step in narrowing down the field of agents in your territory. A good script is direct and to the point. It attracts or repels, allowing you to quickly sort the agents that are a good fit from the agents that are not. Use these scripts as a starting point in your success in recruiting agents to your brokerage.

18

THE FINAL LESSON

I was asked a shocking question by another business owner. It was a question that I didn't have an answer to. One that I hadn't considered before. It was at a business retreat where entrepreneurs all shared their ideas and best practices.

The small group of successful business owners each share about their business and then critique each other's businesses to help them uncover the weaknesses and blindspots in their business plans.

Being new to the group I was asked to give a 45-minute presentation about my brokerage. I proudly shared what we have achieved thus far, the awards and recognition we had garnered, and what my long-term audacious goals were.

Up to that point, I felt I was doing a good job as the head trainer and CEO of my brokerage. We were four years into growing the real estate brokerage. We had four offices, two that were company-owned and two that we had franchised to other agents that wanted to operate their own brokerage. With over $5 million in annual commission income, our sales were strong and for the most part, we were meeting our business objectives.

The business owner who asked the question had a business where she manufactured and sold dog treats… or something. I honestly don't remember. Whatever the case, she was very successful and didn't beat around the bush with her questions.

Each business owner asked a question about the business. When it came to her she paused for a moment, looked me dead in the eyes, and asked, "What's your exit strategy?"

"Exit strategy?" I replied.

"I am planning on doing this forever. I don't need an exit strategy," I said. With a smug grin on my face.

She smiled back. I could tell in that moment that I had walked into a trap.

She then said, "You have investors, right?"

"Yes," I said.

"They want their money back, correct?"

"Of course," I said, thinking to myself: Where is this going?

She then said, "Even if you plan on working until you die, your investors deserve an opportunity to exit. They didn't invest their money to ride it out forever, and even if you plan on working until the end, you and your family should also have an exit strategy."

She continued, "An exit strategy doesn't mean that you must sell or exit. It just means that you could in the event you choose, or it is necessary for the business. Your business plan should reflect built-in exit strategies for you, your partners, and investors. Ideally, the first exit point is within 3-5 years."

I think at this point I looked confused. So, she explained in more detail. "An exit strategy can be positioning the company for a sale or merger, taking the company public, or building the company's savings in order to pay back investors or buy out the founder or a partner. Go back and review your business and come back with a 3-year exit strategy for you and the other key members."

My mind was spinning. How could I have overlooked such an important detail? I thought to myself. We were nearing the end of our fourth year in business and my partner wanted out and my investors were wondering when the business would start paying back their investments. Nevertheless, I took her advice seriously and I set out to find an exit strategy for them and myself.

The experience of building your own business and watching it flourish is only second to seeing your children grow and achieve milestones. You will never forget your baby's first steps or the first time they said Mamma or Daddy.

Like my child, I remember celebrating our first commission check, our first profitable month, and achieving our milestone of 1,000 families served. It is something that you can't experience without doing it. The excitement, fear, and happiness of being an entrepreneur are tangled together so tightly until they are unrecognizable from one another. When I reflect back on that time it feels like one giant ball of emotion.

While completing the task of coming up with an exit strategy, I discovered a flaw in my brokerage's business model. The truth is I always knew that the flaw was there, but I thought I would be able to work around it before it became too big of a problem.

As our brokerage grew and expanded into new locations and then onto franchises it became very clear that this was a bigger challenge to solve than I had prepared for. When I was asked to return to the coaching group with my exit strategy the flaw in my business plan was preventing me from coming up with any reasonable solution.

This mistake was preventing me from creating an exit strategy and it was holding my brokerage back from growing to what it could be. The flaw in the business was... ME!

While the brokerage wasn't supported by my personal sales and personal commission income, I did build it around my coaching knowledge and full-time recruiting efforts. A great friend and mentor shared with me that our greatest strength can also be our greatest weakness. As a teacher at heart, my passion led me to build the entire brokerage with me at the center as the head recruiter, head coach, and head decision-maker.

By the time the brokerage had grown to four locations, I found myself zig-zagging across town from office to office to meet with potential recruits and to coach our top producing agents.

Early in the startup phase of the brokerage, my partners and I knew this wouldn't be scalable, but I believed as time went on, I would be able to find and train other people that were as passionate as I was to help agents grow their business.

After five years and many mis-hires, I had only found one other person with the passion and the skills to recruit and coach agents. The reality was, we were both working endless hours without an end in sight.

This decision was stalling my brokerage growth and I knew I had to find a solution… an Exit Strategy. My brokerage had to change from an immature adolescent that was hanging on their parent's pant leg to an independent adult, or at least an argumentative teenager!

I needed to remove myself from the center of the brokerage, but still support the agents, so my brokerage could continue to grow without me holding it back. With this in mind, I began my search for a solution to remove myself from the dependent role I placed myself in within my brokerage.

There were many options. One option was to scale the business down by closing a few offices to save some money and reorganize the business. The second option was to raise more money so we could add more staff and build a technology solution to support the agents. Another was to sell the brokerage and exit altogether.

By the fifth year of running my brokerage, my last partner had decided to exit and I now had the responsibility of the company entirely on my shoulders. I was desperate for a solution. The best option I could find was to fold my boutique brokerage into a much larger brokerage that had more resources for the agents.

My thought was that this would allow me to stay involved in the day to day operations, get some of my time back, and the agents would have more support from the additional staff and technology that the larger brokerage provided.

It seemed like the perfect solution, but the transition wasn't as smooth as planned. Had I done a better job aligning the Mission, Vision, and Values of my brokerage to the Mission, Vision, and Values of the new brokerage, we would have had better agent retention.

About half of the agents left when the merger was announced and several more departed shortly after. The vision I started with for my brokerage quickly fell apart and within a few short months what was left of my brokerage was gone.

My biggest regret is that it did not have to be this way. Had I started with a better plan, one with the end in mind; an exit strategy for my partners, my investors, and myself. This would have prevented me from building the brokerage around me, and forced me to take the time earlier to find long-term solutions to recruit and coach agents so the business didn't rely so heavily on me.

Maybe it was my own ego that got in the way. Maybe it was a fear of failure, trusting others, or letting go that prevented me from addressing the error in my business plan earlier. Whatever the case, it taught me how crucial an exit strategy is to the longterm success of your brokerage.

The Bottom Line for Your Exit Strategy

If you are currently working on the business plan for your brokerage, don't overlook or underestimate the important step of creating an exit plan for you. This will prevent you from becoming the cog in the wheel of business that prevents your brokerage from growing to its potential.

Your exit strategy will also hold you accountable to your investors, and protect the business if you or your partner(s) wish to move on at some point. Remember, a great business plan starts with the end in mind.